DO WE HAVE A PLACE IN HEAVEN?

Keegan Naidoo

COPYRIGHT PAGE

Scripture quotations marked (WEB) are taken from World English Bible translation. Scripture marked (KJV) are taken from King James Version translation.

Title: Do We Have A Place In Heaven?

ISBN: 978-0-620-96258-2 (print)

ISBN: 978-0-620-96259-9 (e-book)

ISBN: 978-0-620-96260-5 (audio)

Although this publication is designed to provide accurate

DEDICATED TO:

My beloved God who never gets tired to listen to all of my prayers. You are my companion, my creator, and the air that I breathe. I can't see myself still living and fulfilling my dreams without you.

My awesome wife, Maria, who encouraged me to be happier every single day. You are my star who lightens up my life, and cheers me up when the world is trying to dim my shine. Thank you for inspiring me to be the best husband, father, and person that I could ever be.

My son, Elijah, and my nieces, Simone, and Chanelle. I hope and pray for greatness in your life. All of you are undeniably gifts to our family. I can't wish for anything else but a wonderful future waiting for you. May your dreams be fulfilled with the help of our God in heaven.

And lastly, to my loving mum and dad. I'm grateful to have such amazing parents like you. Thank you for taking care of me, and letting me express myself. It helps me to become the man that I always wanted to be.

Table of Contents

PROLOGUE

It is a public knowledge and common understanding that Christians ought to be the followers of Jesus Christ, and be disciplined in teaching and practising the gospel which is the structured teaching in the Bible. Any person or group of people practising, as well as spreading the word outside the paradox of the Bible, is corrupting the faith and deceiving the people seeking salvation and a genuine relationship with God. The gospel of Jesus Christ remains undisputed throughout time by eyewitnesses across different social classes, races, and even religions. The Bible gives an account of the genealogy of mankind, and the specific purpose of Mary, being a virgin and giving birth to Jesus Christ, the saviour of humans, who died on the cross for our sins, was resurrected, and ascended in heaven. Further to this, Jesus warns his followers in the Bible that spiritual leaders will deceive the body of Christ, teach a different gospel, and introduce a different God to advance themselves for their agenda.

This book is dedicated on exposing the kingdom of darkness and their tactics in keeping us away from our relationship with God.

CHAPTER 1

THE DOER OF THE GOSPEL

We are living in this world where huge number of people claimed things that aren't. There was a time when fallacious beliefs were confessed to everyone. The beliefs that are widely known are sporadically helpful to many, but destructive to somebody. It created diversion and confusion, which led, sometimes, to a savage feud over religions.

There are approximately four thousand and three hundred religions all over the world, and only God knows how many secret societies are executing atrocious cruelties which are the roots of horrendous gloom. We cannot deny that these different faith communities cause conflicts between their members and followers. This threatens the future, and subconsciously corrupts the minds of people who only wanted to have relationship with God.

Let's all take a pause and ask ourselves, "What's gonna happen between two people obtruding their two different credence to each other?"

We have to accept the fact that forcing our beliefs to someone will easily generate hatred, and devise diabolical intentions for one another. Maybe, some of you are questioning yourselves right now: "How can different religions subconsciously corrupt and deceive the minds of its worshippers?"

Religions can corrupt the minds of their people through the leaders preaching false beliefs which can cause anger, annoyance, and sometimes, vengeance. These communities are supposed to help us, encourage us to love one another, and lead us to the right path, but there were periods in our lives when they only caused us damage and disfigurement.

Amongst the thousands of religions out there, Christianity holds a vast quantity of devotees; there are two billion Christians all over the world which is thirty percent of the world's population. Christians believe that Jesus Christ was anointed by God as the saviour of mankind.

It is fascinating to hear that Christianity is publicly known. It feels so nice to meet someone who has the same values as you do. It makes you feel free and understood. On the other hand, we mistakenly thought that Christianity has its solidarity or the singleness of purpose on earth, but it is not always like that. Over time, the meaning of Christianity and how Christians are supposed to be are heavily altered. It changed from the beginning of time, and continuously amended until the era of the twenty-first century. We met a lot of people who claimed to be Christians, but vilely do things that were against God's words.

I am not asserting that Christians like me are supposed to be sacred. We all know that each one of us commit sins that, sometimes, we are not even aware of. We are not holy, and we make terrible mistakes, but if we’re gonna describe what followers of Christ mean, we surely understand what are our obligations, and if we actually do things that God wants us to do.

Who Are the Followers of Christ?

If we are going to use our time, and scrutinize God's words, we will perceive that followers of Christ are self-effacing and polite.

A false balance is an abomination to Yahweh, but accurate weights are his delight. When pride comes, then comes shame, but with humility comes wisdom.The integrity of the upright shall guide them, but the perverseness of the treacherous shall destroy them.

(Proverbs 11: 1-3 WEB)

It is incontestable that humbleness is one of the characteristics of a Christian; it represents submissiveness and graciousness in following God's commandments. On the contrary, pride is an egotistic character of human thinking that there is no need for God in our lives. Having pride is also lacking of wisdom. People only rely on themselves, and never want to seek guidance from above.

Further to this, the Bible also talks about followers of Christ who are honest. Living on this earth, and socializing with different people make our lives harder. We have to go through things that are impenetrable to deal with. There is always one situation in our lives that forces us to lie about one particular thing that we don't want to.

Lying lips are an abomination to Yahweh, but those who do the truth are his delight.

(Proverbs 12:22 WEB)

Have you ever met someone who lied in front of your face even though you already knew the truth? How does it feel?

Being lied by someone will never be a good thing. You'll feel dissatisfied, mad, and exasperated. So, what, do you think, God feels every time that we are lying about the things that we shouldn't do?

We meet people who lie about their values in life. We manufacture thousands of stories for our own sake, and we look at lying as an everyday part of our existence. Even the man of the cloth gives us a distorted view of what Christianity is by spreading the so-called "God's words".

These words are twisted and modified for their own interests. Most evangelists of today seek only for financial gains, power, and fame. I am not professing that all of them only want those that I mentioned; it is merely an observation. But If we are going to a deeper side of the World Wide Web, tales about millions of preachers are written. Some committed sexual assault, some are plunderers, and some are murderers.

How can a teacher disseminate God's words, and do

horrid things at the same time? Who can we actually listen to in today's world if the preachers. Themselves, are untrustworthy?

These questions are unreservedly normal. As I mentioned earlier, this kind of deed creates confusion and, from time to time, produces destruction. That's what lying can do to a fellow human being. If humans only have fear and love for our God, then they will not do such actions that are against Him. They said that fearing the Lord God is the beginning of wisdom and knowledge.

Now let's picture it out in our mind. If we have the tenderness and love for our spouse, we will always try our very best not to aggravate our partners, or even the people that matter to us. We have the fear and love for them. It is the same thing when we fear and love the Lord. We have the wisdom to do the right thing, we have the knowledge to act accordingly, and we have the understanding to see the values of each commandment written.

We want to make it comprehensible for everyone. There's no one living in this world who is Holy aside from Lord Jesus Christ. We are not saying that we have to be sacred, righteous and sin-free, but what we are seeking to explain is endeavouring to follow the right instructions will not cost anything, and you'll be the one to gain the benefits in the end. We must realize that knowing God's words will never be enough. It will not suffice God's desire for his followers.

Christians of the twenty-first century should, at least, make an effort not only to read the Bible but also to comprehend and follow what's inside of it. That is why it is written- faith without work is dead. Saying and doing activities are two different things.

Dealing with Non-Believers and Other Religious People

As mentioned a while ago, we will always encounter thousands of people who have different values from us. They become part of our everyday lives, and more often play a very indispensable role to us as human beings. They could be our friends, family, colleagues and relatives. As days go by, we learn to socialize, and accept the unfamiliarity in each one. It became normal for most Christians to shower respect and love for one another. However, it is not always the case for the reason that, sooner or later, our respect and understanding for another person who has disparate spiritual beliefs will be tested and short-lived. Unexpectedly, time will come when we're gonna ask ourselves, "How am I going to deal with non-believers?"

First of all, what does non-believer mean?

A non-believer is a person who lacks belief in and idea about God or a religion. In a broader sense, it is a deprivation of faith in the actuality of the deity, or the divine being.

During interaction with those non-believers, and people who have different religious duties, it is common to have occasional contretemps that lead to war of words. It is vital for Christians like us to gain understanding of how to handle the situation of incompatibility.

So then, as we have opportunity, let's do what is good toward all men, and especially toward those who are of the household of the faith.

(Galatians 6:10 WEB)

Having interrelationships to people who are not believers of Christ can be thorny; it can be stressful, baffling and frustrating. In spite of that, reminding ourselves that we are called to love and encourage the serenity of our existence as individuals can undeniably help us to administer the difficulty.

As a matter of fact, you don't need to be a Christian to have respect for other's freedom of choice. Even God bestowed us liberty and free will to choose him or not. Moreover, showing consideration or sensitivity while socialising with different types of people with different faith and thinking will also be useful in alleviating the problem.

We have to learn to treat each one of us, Christians or not, with civility and respect. Apart from this, having consideration and thoughtfulness about somebody else's belief must not make you embrace and accept their teachings as your own. God's words are clearly warning us about working with others that can prevent us from undertaking the work that Jesus Christ wants us to do, or having a relationship with people who force us to carry out things that are not in a righteous instruction.

If you still can't understand, let's take things more straightforwardly.

Try to imagine that you worked in a place which is known to be moral and ethical. As you performed your duty in that place, you found yourself growing and doing better day by day. You became confident, happy and humble. However, your superior put you in an entirely different place, and asked you to do the same thing; clearly, you cannot do anything but accept it. While working in that new place, you felt that it was absolutely contradicting from where you were before. You were then encircled by people who do not believe as you do, and whose domination was damaging your faith and morality. Some were doing sexual immorality, the others were swallowed by greed, some were wrathful and envious. You stayed in that place for quite a long time, and one day, you noticed that it was already affecting you tremendously as a person. You were no longer happy because you were full of rage, you were no longer humble because you turned prideful, and you were no longer confident as you became greedy and envious. You looked around, and saw others who seemed to be fine. They never changed, and they simply continued their lives as if no one was influencing them. Finally, you decided to run out of that place and never look back. From that moment, you felt the freedom and the peace inside you; it made you glad that you were able to go out from that surroundings, and gradually redeemed yourself again.

As I mentioned earlier, you cannot do anything, but accept the order of your superior to move you to a different place. I want you to understand that it is the same thing as having a relationship with different types and kinds of people; you will not be able to choose who you want to interact with as people come and go.

Moreover, working in an unethical place with people having immoral behaviour can cause you two things. Firstly, it can affect you horribly as a person; it can badly dominate and turn you into a completely outrageous being. You can do the things that they are doing, and their influence may cause you harm. On the other hand, keeping yourself in that same place will test your loyalty. It will check your commitment and your devotion on your faith, values in life, constancy as a Christian, as well as your morality as a human.

In the end, we have the freedom to choose for ourselves. Do you want to go out from that place filled with wickedness, or are you gonna stay, believing that you are strong enough to hold out against the sinful way?

No temptation has taken you except what is common to man.

God is faithful, who will not allow you to be tempted above what you are able, but will with the temptation also make the way of escape, that you may be able to endure it.

(1 Corinthians 10:13 WEB)

CHAPTER 2

THE CHILDREN OF GOD AND THEIR ENVIRONMENT

Raising a child at this current time will never be easy. Many people said that the world turns upside down, and thinking about raising a human being will only be a selfish act to do. I encounter and meet a lot of people who never plan to have a child, and some don't want to raise a family at all. We often think that it is a completely self-centred behaviour; we assume that they only think about the struggles of having a family, and not the bright side of it. There are only few people who tried to acknowledge one-s logical thought.

While growing up in an unsophisticated living, I witnessed my flesh and blood raising their children and building a family. I saw them doing their utmost to elevate their situation the best possible way they can. I am one of the breathing testimonies of how each of them wrestled in life. I watched them providing the needs of their children at such a young age. I observed the parents giving their very best for their treasured child, but in the end, their offspring were eaten by the earth; their cherished children are now doing fleshly and worldly craft.

At the time of my youth, I told myself that I would never be ready to have a family. I once said to everyone that I was not getting a glimpse of my future having a child. I was fine to be alone. I was frightened to have a responsibility while living on this earth. I was scared that I would not be able to handle a covenant that God designed for us, aside from the fact that I was also damaged by what I witnessed in my family. The reality of life injured me and forced me to think differently. I was shaped to become a man-child who refused to grow and didn't want the future that God has to offer me. I was haunted by the dreadful happenings in each one of us, and I never wanted to pass it to my bloodline.

In others words, I had the same way of reasoning as the others. I also didn't want to do anything about raising a home. I never gave myself a chance to look and see the good side of it. Nonetheless, everything changed when I sought for intellectual acuity to God. I prayed night and day for Him to show me the light and the right path that I should follow.

Not long ago when God answered my prayers; he

allowed me to see the dazzling part of life that has been missing in me. One day, I just saw myself praying onto my knees, and asking for forgiveness for all of the things that I have done. From that time, I requested a gift from God; I demanded to have an offspring, and he immediately responded to me with an amazing touch.

God blessed them. God said to them, "Be fruitful, multiply, fill the earth, and subdue it. Have dominion over the fish of the sea, over the birds of the sky, and over every living thing that moves on the earth."

(Genesis 1:28 WEB)

If you are one of those people who are highly strung and anxious, I want you to know that I've also been there, and I've done that. There's nothing wrong with being worried about the things that we cannot control. I know the feeling of anxiety to raise a kid or to handle a home while living in this world where most people are doing horrifying things. I can sense the struggle in your mind thinking about how you're gonna protect the people you love.

First of all, I want you to understand that you will never be able to protect the people that matter to you if you don't know what and who can harm them. Are we sure that only the world outside can control and destroy them, or didn't we just realise that even the people that surround us can hold the greatest influence over our loved ones?

The Child Is Given to the Family

Many people believe that when a new life arises, hope will follow. We usually hear that having a child is a blessing from God, time after time. Christians and other members of different faith communities believe that a newborn must be dedicated to God; they said that the child must be raised in a Godly environment, and work in the direction that comes from the Lord. However, how can we raise a child in our home where there are family members whose values are different from ours?

A lot of things are happening in our surroundings, and we, as parents, are striving to teach our children the right way. We encourage them to do things that we think are right and best for them. We are praying for knowledge and strength to help them, and bending our knees to the Lord to give them a gleaming life. It is natural for everyone to think for the best for their children. We build plans for them, and sometimes, we are so excited to see what kind of future awaits our fruits. All that we want to do is to protect them from all the distractions on earth.

Surprisingly, not everything would happen as planned.

At times, our best-loved child would never become the person that we always wanted him to be, to the point that we would ask ourselves where did we go wrong.

It seems like our lives have fallen apart knowing that our children are not on the right path. They are into the mundane world and unspiritual acts. We started to question God why our prayers have not been answered, when in fact, we are the ones who made all these terrible blunders. We are so occupied in protecting our family outside, but we forgot that there are also people that can influence them inside, hiding in plain sight.

It slipped in our minds that all human beings who surround our family can affect them unfavourably, until it's too late. They already broadened their immoral views, passed their questionable faith to our children, and infected our family with their unethical beliefs. All the sacrifices, prayers, and tears that we shed for our loved ones turned into sorrow because we failed to see who's in front of us.

We must always remember that the environment where we are living in today holds the greatest impact on us, and everyone else.

Do you still believe that it is only the outside world, or

did we just fail to see who's inside our home?

All your children will be taught by Yahweh; and your children's peace will be great.

(Isaiah 54:13 WEB)

Where Can Our Child Learn aside from Home?

It became a norm to every parent to send their children to school. We were conditioned to think that a learning institution is one of the harmless places on earth where we can leave our children without fear; we grew up thinking that school is the second home for our kids. However, there was a time when I questioned myself where we got the guts to trust strangers to look after our precious children. We freed ourselves from the suspicion that our little one will be in harm. We let them go at such a young age, hoping that they will grow up into graceful humans, and that they will find what they want in life.

While reading and watching documentaries about the centre of learning, I realised that school isn't always the safe place for our child, nor for anyone else. The reality of life while living on this earth pushes us more to the edge of terror. We get worried about our family, and we, oftentimes, overthink and ask, what if our daughters or our sons will be next?

Next on what?

If we are gonna visit the news on World Wide Web, watch thousands of videos on televisions, and even listen to our radio, we rarely hear horror stories about learners, and the perilous things that involve them. Sadly, no matter how seldom it is, it is still existing, and it can happen to you, or to everyone.

Some horrifying truths are not even disclosed just to keep the honourable name of the institution.

There was a time in our lives when, just after we got up from bed, and turned our radio on, we heard something that destroyed our morning; it was a news about a student who died for an unknown reason. It could be a drug overdose or homicide.

The next day, as we were peacefully sitting on the lounge, facing the television, a news popped up on the screen. We just took a deep breath and said, "It happened again."

A body was found floating in the river; it was the body of a missing child. The parents said that their child never made it home after school. They waited for so long, but their child never came. We didn't know the cause of the tragic demise, but theories were playing in our heads; it can be murder, suicide, or even bullying that turned into loss of life. No one really knew.

It is absolutely normal for parents like me to get frightened. I am scared about two things: it's either my child will be found breathless, or my child will be the one to take the life.

How are we gonna train our child to be both soft and tough at the same time?

We might think that raising children is hard, but for me, raising them to be well-mannered is harder; it takes a lot of courage and understanding.

Train up a child in the way he should go, and when he is old he will not depart from it.

(Proverbs 22:6 WEB)

I mentioned so many times before that it was not only the outside world that can harm our children. Our beloved family can influence and train them in a way that you never wanted them to be. On top of that, we failed to look closely at what might happen to them at their so-called "second home".

We have faith that they will be great, and that they will be taken cared of there, but we're wrong. I am not saying that every school is a dangerous place for them, or that every school has been played by life and death. What I am trying to clarify is that we cannot put our brimming confidence that they will become the person that God wants them to be.

We must realize that the medium of learning at home is different from that in the learning institution. We are striving every single time to show our kids what we know is right, but some things may change as they go outside. We cannot control who's gonna be with them, or who's gonna teach them; all that we can do is to bend our knees and pray that they will be protected every second of their lives.

For God didn't give us a spirit of fear, but of power, love, and self-control.

(2 Timothy 1:7 WEB)

They might teach things to our children which are far from what we taught them. They might mould their innocent minds to think irrationally, and they might change their views about what is right and what is wrong. We, however, are the parents; we can do anything if we seek guidance. We have the intelligence and strength which come from our God.

Let them go out and see the world, let them open their eyes for them to see what is on earth, and let them walk through their own feet. Have faith that they will have protection, have faith with your night and day prayers, and have faith that you did your best for them. You helped them in knowing diligently the word of the divine being, and at the end of the line, they will surely learn how to help themselves. They will bow and humble themselves for God to favour them.

I'm gonna ask you, and answer it by your heart, "To whom are you gonna put your overflowing trust?"

"Behold, I send you out as sheep among wolves. Therefore be wise as serpents and harmless as doves.

(Matthew 10:16 WEB)

CHAPTER 3

THE STAGES OF LIFE

While growing up, I was always being taught about the difference between children and adults. I made a lot of mistakes in the past because of lack of understanding on the differences between childhood and adulthood. I know that most of us behave in a way that old-aged people will definitely question our parents' way of raising a child.

The silly part is that, in my whole life, I wasn't able to comprehend how an adult and a child should act. Even I, as a grown-up man, behave like a teenager, and think that I am still young. I don't know how to differentiate people's behaviours and ways of thinking based on the stages of life. Maybe, that's the reason why my mum and dad had a hard time taking care of me. They tried to nurture me, but I was still young and naive to discern things on this earth; thus, it never last. While looking back and thinking about what I did, I considered myself a halfwit, not until I had my own family, specifically, a child.

I saw lots of kids who appeared to be so rude in front of

many people by acting and talking like an adult. Then I asked myself, “How am I going to teach my child to be sharp-witted on this earth? How will my child remain innocent, but mindful, at the same time, without disrespecting others?”

But first, before thinking about how children, teens, and adults are supposed to be, let's find out what stages of life is all about.

The stages of life are sequences of changes. These refer to major reshaping of an organism from one stage to another. Every creature on earth that was made by God has its own phase and cycle. Each one of us who are still living on earth has been through so much within the period of our very own existence. We will never experience the second stage without having the familiarity and understanding of the first stage. In the other words, we cannot be a teenager without being an infant.

Stages of Human Life

Infancy to Childhood:

Infancy to childhood is the earliest stage in a person's life. It is the moment in a living being from birth to age eight. Women give birth to a child that is naturally vulnerable and infirm. This period in a human life needs more attention and care than the rest of the other stages. Over and above that, kids are more intelligent than we think. They create adorable sounds to communicate with us; they cry, they smile, they feel things as normal people do, and, often times, imitate our actions. Our little ones innocently emulate our behaviour as their pattern or model. Not one day in my life that I gave credence to someone who told me how babies can be smart, until I witnessed it myself.

My question is, if children are taking us as their examples, then how can we make ourselves better for them to have good role models?

Even a child makes himself known by his doings, whether his work is pure, and whether it is right.

(Proverbs 20:11 WEB)

Most Christian families look after their kids based on God's instructions. We seek guidance to the point that we are kneeling down to the Lord to hear our prayers. Having children is like having a piece of your soul, walking and wandering outside of you. It is full of rich emotions. There's a lot of happiness, adversity, unpredictability, and sometimes, doubt.

God's words are filled with wisdom and knowledge about parenting that we can use in times of precariousness. We, as parents, can't promise that we can always stand still for our family; each one of us knows that time will come when we'll feel the lack of certainty about rearing our own child.

They were also bringing their babies to him, that he might touch
them. But when the disciples saw it, they rebuked them. **16** *Jesus*
summoned them, saying, "Allow the little children to come to
me, and don't hinder them, for God's Kingdom belongs to such
as these. **17** *Most certainly, I tell you, whoever doesn't receive*
God's Kingdom like a little child, he will in no way enter into

it."

(Luke 18: 15-17 WEB)

The first thing that we can do is to look at ourselves, and see if we need to change. We are the models of our daughters and sons, and if we can't make better adjustments to our permutable way of acting and habits, then we cannot expect our children to practice greater things. In simple words, it all starts with us.

Every morning, we are always seeing our child singing and watching cartoons on television. Then and now, we unknowingly chant to the music as the shows start; we just simply got used to it, and subconsciously programmed our minds. We cannot deny that the few hours of cartoons or animated films help us to do things in the house, and even for ourselves. We let our child watch their favourite tv shows for almost a day in order for us to finish things that don't even really matter; this is the downfall of living in the era of 21st Century.

From time to time, most of us choose to hand over a gadget to our children for them to get entertained and amused, instead of building a strong and valuable foundation that they can use while growing up. On the contrary, I can never blame the parents for this. Not all of us have the ability to spend time with our children because of the whole day strenuous work. There's a father who needs to wake up at six in the morning to get ready for work, and perform his never-ending duties. The mother, who stays in the house, needs to do her ongoing commitment from morning 'til night. Some of us probably have a day to rest only, yet we need to check and read our emails, as well as paperwork. We choose to use our rest day to finish our remaining jobs. In some cases, both parents seek employment to sustain the necessity of each one. Their child is then left in the hands of a stranger; they have no choice but to trust other people in instilling good values to their beloved child.

We can only do one thing at a time, and that's the fact. We cannot put our presence in front of our children while doing important things for our family. However, we can always seek guidance, not from anyone else but the Divine Being.

Rather than putting cartoons that might influence our kids negatively, which may lead them to having violent behaviour, let us try to introduce to them TV shows that are gospel-based, and meant for kids. There are hundreds of videos about the Bible that you and your child can watch. If our actions can change, you can surely raise your child in a Godly manner.

In addition to that, instead of doing your job at home on your rest day, I advise you to leave your duties to your workplace, and fulfil your role as a parent to your child. You must always remember that you only have few days of spending time with your loved ones, so be sure that you make the best out of it. Leave at work the things that belong to work, and give to your family what belongs to them.

It is vain for you to rise up early, to stay up late, eating the bread of toil, for he gives sleep to his loved ones.

(Psalm 127:2 WEB)

Puberty to Adulthood:

Puberty to adulthood is a phase in the life of human beings which starts in teenage years and ends in the thirties. It is the condition of being fully grown, physically and mentally. At this time, parents lose parental rights and responsibilities to their own kids. They are finally at their legal age, and therefore, consider themselves independent and self-reliant. But as guardians, we constantly feel anxious for our children. We overthink and trouble our minds thinking about the situation that they are facing. Regardless of how fearful we are for our child's life and decision making, we are only capable of educating them; we can only impart knowledge to them which they can use until the day that you depart from this world.

As I mentioned, only God can help us find a way in teaching our daughters and sons.

And you shall teach them diligently to your children, and shall talk of them when you sit in your house, and when you walk by the way, and when you lie down, and when you rise up.

(Deuteronomy 6:7 WEB)

In their teenage years, it is very important for us to play our part as a mother or a father. We must communicate with our children for the reason that they will learn things from you, and from the people around them. They say that adolescence is the most crucial stage, not only for children, but also for their guardians. Teens are fragile and can get easily influenced by their peers, family members, and even strangers; that's when they gain understanding about the outside world. And if we failed to at least make an effort to guide them, it can cause destruction of their future.

We cannot hold our children's future; no one is sure about the life that awaits them, but we are trying our very best to give great lessons, wisdom, and fate that we think they truly need. But how are we gonna do it?

Once your child hit the stage when they need to go and experience things outside, we must teach them to be watchful over the people that surround them. They have to be smart in choosing friends and partners. Peers are one the biggest contributors pertaining to our child's behaviour. We have to ensure that our son's or daughter's companion will not be an ill wind that blows no good to anybody.

But as it is, I wrote to you not to associate with anyone who is called a brother who is a sexual sinner, or covetous, or an idolater, or a slanderer, or a drunkard, or an extortionist. Don't even eat with such a person.

(1 Corinthians 5:11 WEB)

Over the succeeding years of their teenage life, we instantly feel the tranquility knowing that our children managed to defeat the unacceptable impact of atrocious human behaviour. Now, they are ready to build their own family, raise their own kids, and experience the same feeling that we felt for them. We are just genuinely and truly proud to watch the gleaming adventure of our own children.

However, our role as parents will never come to an end there. We will still witness our sons or daughters tying the knot with their life partners. All that we can do is to pray, night and day, that they make right decisions for themselves and for others that may adversely be affected.

Sadly, our best-loved child needs to separate his or her way from us. Our time on this earth will then be counted, our light that once gleams like the beautiful sun is slowly fading, and our breathing days will soon become a distant memory.

Middle Age to Old Age

Middle age to old age is the last stage of a human. This

is the period when people usually settle down with their respective partners, and wait for their bodies to shrink and wrinkle. This is the time when they are patiently counting the days of their lives. At this moment, each and every one of us look back and reflect on our life's disappointments and fulfilment.

If our children reach this stage, we are probably lying underneath the soil of the earth, or we might still be breathing, but behaving like an infant; we barely remember things, even our fondest memories, and our bones become weaker than what we could ever imagine.

Our only support is our children and grandchildren whom we guided until the last strength of our body just for them to reach their impressive destinations. It is the time that our offspring will show their patience, love, and care towards us.

We are already old, and can hardly move and even recall things, but if there's one day that we can remember all of the teachings and sacrifices that we have done for our children, we can say to ourselves that everything has paid off. We, as parents, must be proud of what we did; we've spoken never-ending prayers, we continuously seek guidance to our Lord, and our children are now doing the same thing.

We will then close our eyes, appreciating God for giving us a wonderful life.

You will come to your grave in a full age, like a shock of grain comes in its season.

(Job 5:26 WEB)

CHAPTER 4

WATCHES OF FAITH

Many years ago, I was a dedicated member of a church in our town. I would sing, pray, and sit for the whole day because I felt that I was having a relationship with God. It made me feel valued; it gave me energy and unexplainable happiness within my heart. However, years went by, and the energy that I once felt started to disappear. The gladness in my heart faded, and the self-value that I built for years crashed.

Maybe some of you are asking me right now, "How come that I lose myself while being in the presence of God?"

It's been a long time since I questioned myself with the same uncertainty, and I was happy that in the fullness of time, I got an answer.

I was brought up in a Christian home, and my parents had strong Christian values. Mum and dad always wanted me to be with them every time they were clapping their hands, worshipping God when I was little. When I reached my teenage life, I eventually had my own freedom; I could decide for myself if I wanted to join Sunday reverence or not.

As I got older and attained my early twenties, my family still encouraged me to go to church with them, and without hesitation, I did. At first, I had a nice time spent with different people; moreover, I could feel the enjoyment of doing things for the so-called house of God.

In spite of that, it is not long ago when I started seeing improbable things inside of the house where people pray and cry. I gradually questioned myself, and everything that surrounded me.

There's something inside the church that made me tremble. I thought I was the only one, but I was wrong. I spoke to hundreds of people who witnessed and felt the same thing that I had. Their reasons for living in the church were the same rational thoughts that I've been keeping.

To make things clear, I just wanted you to know that I am not against the churches, or ministers of religions all over the world; I am just not in favour of the pastors who use the house of the Divine Creator to scheme worshippers, exploit proceeds, and conduct unethical behaviours. These teachers' actions are clearly at odds with the interest of Christianity. I am not encouraging all of you to start hatred against religions nor priests; instead, I am here to inspire every one to listen and look very carefully about the things that are being taught inside your beloved church.

The first noticeable thing, not only for me but for the huge number of people, is the contribution that comes from each member of the faith communities. There are thousands of claims and accusations from former members of different religious groups stating that the church leader was forcing the people within the community to give tithes and financial offerings. We must understand that it doesn't only happen to Christianity; this kind of strict enforcement is continuously occurring to thousands of religions all over the world.

Let each man give according as he has determined in his heart, not grudgingly or under compulsion, for God loves a cheerful giver.

(2 Corinthians 9:7 WEB)

Before we start discussing one of the controversial topics

of the 21st century, let me define what is tithing, and what is offering.

In Hebrew, the word tithe means tenth. Tithing is the tenth part of your earnings that is supposedly allocated for your church. In Leviticus 27:30, it is said that,

And all the tithe of the land, whether of the seed of the land or of the fruit of the tree, is the Lord's: it is holy unto the Lord.

Offerings, on the other hand, are known as gifts that are handed over, aside from tithing. In other words, offering is whatever extra that you present with.

So, “Are members of the church obliged to tithe?” This is question that has been circulating for many years.

The straight answer is no, as Christians of the new generation are not mandated to do the ten-percent contribution.

In the Old Testament, tithing is mandated to support Godly ordinance and people who are in need namely: foreigners, widows and orphans.

At the end of every three years, you shall bring all the tithe of your increase in the same year, and shall store it within your gates. 29 The Levite, because he has no portion nor inheritance with you, as well as the foreigner living among you, the fatherless, and the widow who is within your gates shall come, and shall eat and be satisfied; that Yahweh your God may bless you in all the work of your hand which you do.

(Deuteronomy 14: 28-29 WEB)

The foremost motive for the Old Testament to permit tithe is already over and done since Jesus Christ sacrificed Himself on the cross, and gave up his life to fulfil the law and be the saviour of humankind. In the New Testament, Jesus never intended to subvert the proposition of tithing, instead, He determined the things that shouldn't be neglected that will help man to obtain salvation aside from tithing.

Woe to you, scribes and Pharisees, hypocrites! For you tithe mint, dill, and cumin,[a] and have left undone the weightier matters of the law: justice, mercy, and faith. But you ought to have done these, and not to have left the other undone.

(Matthew 23:23 WEB)

On top of all of these, the Bible still talks about giving in a Godly manner. Giving should be carried out cheerfully, voluntarily, humbly and generously. We must always be aware that tithing is supposed to be open-handed, blissful and not compulsory. It must be coming from our hearts without grudge and hesitation, without fear and guilt.

Financial offerings, tithing and materialistic gift giving will not save us from all our wrongdoings; we will not be cursed by not giving money that we don't even have to pastors and churches. In Galatians 3:13, it is understandably written that,

Christ hath redeemed us from the curse of the law, being made a curse for us: for it is written, Cursed is every one that hangeth on a tree:

If Jesus Christ saved us from the curse of the law, then it

is clear that we will not be cursed for not tithing.

No one must force us to do something that we can't; we must give with a good heart and loving mind.

Another controversial account that many believers are questioning about enforcing financial contributions is the lavish lifestyle of the preachers. Thousands of preachers have been called out for having a luxurious and expensive manner of living. Most of them own mansions which cost millions, move from one place to another using their private jets as well as helicopters, and have extravagant protection. Isn't it written that the gifts, tithes, and offers from believers are supposed to be allocated for people in need, such as strangers, widows, and orphans? Does it not make sense to give something to those humans who are underprivileged?

Sell that which you have, and give gifts to the needy. Make for yourselves purses which don't grow old, a treasure in the heavens that doesn't fail, where no thief approaches, neither moth destroys. 34 *For where your treasure is, there will your heart be also.*

(Luke 12:33-34 WEB)

Many of these leaders explained that they never touched the contribution of the members for their living. They insisted that they have their own money to spend for their own needs.

Yet, if these claimed preachers are actually squandering the silver that is meant for good works, then it is between him and God. In Luke 9:3-2, it is distinctly said that;

And he said unto them, take nothing for your journey, neither staves, nor scrip, neither bread, neither money; neither have two coats apiece.

I am not writing to wage war, or attack all of the evangelists, pastors, priests and even the beliefs of each one of us. I am here to stand for those people who were abused by the leaders who used their power to accomplish their inward-looking thoughts.

What then is my reward? That when I preach the Good News, I may present the Good News of Christ without charge, so as not to abuse my authority in the Good News.

(1 Corinthians 9:18 WEB)

Aside from the costly way of living of pastors all over the world, there is one more scandalous issue that they have been facing, now and then. There are disturbingly thousands of complaints and stories against leaders of different religions which are mostly about their sexual violation towards the members of their church. Many worshipers left their beliefs because of this dishonourable matter. A huge number of witnesses can stand to speak the truth about the darkness happening behind the high walls of the Kirk.

Based on their stories, some of the preachers of today took advantage of their position to harm their members who are weak and vulnerable for their own pleasures. There are thousands of young and innocent people who started a grievance against their leader who sexually harassed them. Most of them are fearful about their life and choose to be quiet for many years, until they got the courage to speak up.

Just try to visualise these. What will you feel if, one day, you found out that the same pastor, who is teaching in front of you pertaining to God's words, is connected to some disreputable acts? What will you feel if your innocent children go to the same church where a sordid accusation against the leader is spreading? Will your eyes still be closed, or will you seek guidance from God to show you what is right?

I hope that you realised that these kinds of leaders are dangerous for the new generation; a great number of young people can easily be influenced by their immoralities. We have to seek guidance from no man, but with one God who gives us life.

I wrote to you in my letter to have no company with sexual
sinners; **10** *yet not at all meaning with the sexual sinners of this*
world, or with the covetous and extortionists, or with idolaters;
for then you would have to leave the world. **11** *But as it is, I*
wrote to you not to associate with anyone who is called a
brother who is a sexual sinner, or covetous, or an idolater, or a
slanderer, or a drunkard, or an extortionist. Don't even eat with
such a person.

(1 Corinthians 5:9-11 WEB)

If God said that we mustn't even eat with greedy and

sexually immoral people, then why can't we open our eyes to see what is actually happening inside our own church? Why can't we be the ones to stop these horrible people from victimising blameless human beings? Why do we have to wait for the truth to be revealed?

If God said that we can't even be by them, then why are we still sitting and listening to them, like there is nothing wrong? When are we gonna have the strength to oppose these preachers who use their power to control us

A true witness delivereth souls: but a deceitful witness speaketh lies.

(Proverbs 14:25 KJV)

We can't escape from the fact that all these wrongful acts are happening, even today. We are living in a world where greed and power are more important than saving our souls. Being ignorant of something that is consequential will not be a blissful thing to do. As Christians in the 21st Century, we want to help others, and give our very best to let people understand that there is always harm everywhere, which can be inflicted not only by strangers, but also by people whom we unfailingly regard as a trustee of the gospel.

These are the things that ye shall do; Speak ye every man the truth to his neighbour; execute the judgment of truth and peace in your gates:

(Zechariah 8:16 KJV)

CHAPTER 5

SINS AND VICES

It is a human nature to defend ourselves from something that is harming us. Our first instinct is to always fight the battle that we can see; on the other hand, how we are going to protect ourselves against the unseen spiritual forces seem to be a tough task. How can we win a fight if it is an unseen battle?

In this chapter, I want to elaborate how obscure wickedness changes our life, and affect us in a dreadful way.

We, probably, have experienced thousands of horrible situations throughout our lifetime- circumstances that are truly enigmatic and unexplainable. Most of us were raised in this world believing in a fortunate or an unlucky day; hence, we normally look at our incompetent day as one of the unfortunate scenarios in our life.

However, experiencing infelicitous occurrences is not always the case. We have to think deeper about how things can just happen in a blink of an eye and, turn them into worst nightmare for each of us.

When a person decided to accept our Lord Jesus Christ as his saviour, spiritual warfare is becoming more vehement; it becomes more intense. We might not even know, but evilness in this world is trying to take us to their path, and test our faith.

But how do these deceiving spirits tempt us with the earthly things that we desire the most?

First and foremost, these demonic forces use strategies for us to fall into their trap. Their tactics are to ruin the life that our Lord made for us. It can happen anywhere and to anyone. They are manipulating us to do sins that we are not even aware of. We, as children of God, are unknowingly making transgressions every single day, and thinking that what we are doing pleases God, but we are wrong.

9 The great dragon was thrown down, the old serpent, he who is called the devil and Satan, the deceiver of the whole world. He was thrown down to the earth, and his angels were thrown down with him.

3 and cast him into the abyss, and shut it, and sealed it over him, that he should deceive the nations no more, until the thousand years were finished. After this, he must be freed for a short time.

[8] and he will come out to deceive the nations which are in the four corners of the earth, Gog and Magog, to gather them together to the war; the number of whom is as the sand of the sea.

(Revelation 12:9; 20:3, 8 WEB)

It is normal for everybody to seek knowledge when it comes to the things in this world; we never wanted to be left behind when it comes to news, technology and somebody else's life. We thought that having such kind of awareness will help us in a certain way. It is the same thing with knowing our enemies while breathing on top of the earth's soil. Having an understanding of how devils work will help us not only for today, but for our eternal life. We could save ourselves, and the people that we love. In 2 Corinthians 2:11, it says,

"Lest Satan should get an advantage of us: for we are not ignorant of his devices."

We should not be ignorant about the acts of the enemies. These ungodly spirits will not likely take advantage of us because we have guidance, not from a man, but from God.

The People's Vices

Partners and Friends

People everywhere choose to have a companion than to be alone; having someone on our side gives us a sense of security. We make friends, build long-lasting relationships, and eventually, wish to settle down. We seem so happy about the company that we strengthen, and we end up letting our guards down because we're comfortable with them.

As the days pass by, we never realise that the same people around us, whom we consider as friends or family, are doing terrible acts to destroy us. We stopped being alert, and that's how difficulties started.

These hidden malevolent forces are working every second for the destruction of humanity. They use our companions, friends, and even family to push us to the gloomy side of the world. Yet, how do all of these works?

We must always remember that Satan is the father of lies; he attacks when we least expect it. Satan shows us temptation by the image of our closest ally.

He uses our friends to influence us to do things that can

hurt our family, and can affect our behaviour as trying humans; we are trying to do good to be the better versions of ourselves. For instance, our dearest friends or colleagues influence us to lie in front of our spouse, and they make it seem normal. They are asking us to stay late at night, and spend our time drinking. And, in the worst case, they are pushing us to believe that it's totally fine to check someone else while being with our husband or wife.

Be not deceived: evil communications corrupt good manners.

(1 Corinthians 15:33 KJV)

Sometimes our colleagues are maliciously putting us in trouble at work so that we can lose our job- the work that we need to provide for our family. Moreover, our friends who use to smile at us are also the ones who secretly drag us down in plain sight. Our partners are also being used by these wicked beings. They use our husbands or our wives to put us down. The one whom we chose to be part of our soul can also shatter our existence by making us feel that we are worthless, or by driving our sanity to do hideous conduct. Our cherished families who are away from the presence of God continuously manipulate our way of thinking about how life is supposed to be.

All of these things are not new. Adam and Eve, both were created by God, were also victims of Satan. Sin separates us from our marriage and friends, He can whisper in our ears, and tempt us to do unrighteous deeds.

He that walketh with wise men shall be wise: but a companion of fools shall be destroyed. (Proverbs 13:20 KJV)

That's the reason why it is very important to choose and look closely those who surround us. It is beneficial for us to choose a true and loving company because they will lead us to no destruction, but to good things on earth.

[1] Blessed is the man that walketh not in the counsel of the ungodly, nor standeth in the way of sinners, nor sitteth in the seat of the scornful.

[6] For the Lord knoweth the way of the righteous: but the way of the ungodly shall perish.

(Psalm 1:1,6 KJV)

Drugs and Alcohol Abuse

As I mentioned a while ago, our companions can easily influence us. We might think that they can only manipulate our existence when it comes to lying away from our sight. But how about the behaviours that we consider as perfectly normal, like drinking and more?

In 1 Peter 5:8, it states,

[8] Be sober, be vigilant; because your adversary the devil, as a roaring lion, walketh about, seeking whom he may devour:

Before we start, I don't want anyone of you to feel that I am blaming friends and families for our own sins. However, my written work aims to show you the duties and efforts of the devil which we never see. I am here to encourage you to open your eyes, and act accordingly about your own life. We are not holding anyone accountable for the things that we do, instead, we are trying to show each one of you that there's always a way to recognise the evil in a saint's voice. As is it written: resist the devil, and he will flee.

Worldwide, there are about 3 million individuals passing away each year due to alcohol abuse, and there are approximately a million people who died because of the harmful use of Drugs.

We have to set aside the fact that most of them who lost their lives while consuming dangerous pills are only helpless human beings. If you're gonna do a deeper understanding and research about this matter, you will realise that the huge number of them suffered from mental health problems, and it clearly needs attention.

The ones that endure pain, and eventually lost their breath on earth because of drugs are not always into substance abused, since some are taking them for medication. Most of these humans live through illnesses and diseases, and their last hope to feel well and be better is by using drugs which eventually led to their death.

But how about the rest of mankind who uses these substances for their own rapture?

I witnessed many of my friends who can drink like there is no tomorrow. It is common for me to ask them what urged them to drink early in the morning, every single day. Their answers left me speechless. They would always tell me that their body is craving for it and they are continuously doing it for their own pleasure. They wanted to please their minds, without even thinking that they are slowly ruining their bodies.

That's how the Devil works into our life; he whispers in our ears for our own devastation. I heard lots of stories about young individuals whose lives were already ruined because of drugs. If you will take time to listen to their stories, you will definitely hear the word "friend". It is like a continuous disease can be passed to one another. Some of our friends convinced us to try it once, and then, our body didn't want to stop hungering for such things. If we only know who or what is the enemy, God will help and can assure us that we will be saved.

And be not drunk with wine, wherein is excess; but be filled with the Spirit;

(Ephesians 5:18 KJV)

Lust and Affairs

Infidelity is the number one reason why marriage is falling apart in today's world. It ruins the vow between the couple, and breaks the freedom of suspicion to one another. It leads to divorce, and causes misery, not only to both parties, but also to the children who are involved.

But before that, what does affair really mean?

Affair is an intimate relationship, or a passionate friendship in which one or both participants involved are already married. It all started from having a desire for someone else, aside from your spouse. It can happen everywhere; it could be in our workplaces, leisure places, and even churches.

Hebrew 13:4 says,

"Marriage is honourable in all, and the bed undefiled: but whoremongers and adulterers God will judge."

How do some people end up in a situation like this?

Infidelity can happen because of three possible reasons: unhappy marriage, social pressure, or seduction by the darkness.

When individuals are in an unreconcilable union or unhappy marriage, it is so easy for Satan to control their mind, and overpower their will to do and choose good things. Evil spirits use our environment to harm us in a way that we don't even expect. This wickedness uses our social group to influence us to do horrible behaviour, like sexual immorality.

Demons are really good at doing their job; They are here on earth to destroy and cause only harm. Their task is not to do ethical things, but spoliation. He can place hundreds of images in front of us that we always desire; it can be a beautiful woman, or an inveigler man. From time to time, we feel lustfulness or sensuality to others, but we don't sense the same thing to our own husband or wife. Sins move us apart from our loved ones. If you don't know who's the enemy, then there is a bigger chance for you to fall into the trap- the trap that is meant to demolish your family and your life.

"3 For this is the will of God, even your sanctification, that ye should abstain from fornication:

[4] That every one of you should know how to possess his vessel in sanctification and honour;

[5] Not in the lust of concupiscence, even as the Gentiles which know not God:"

(1 Thessalonians 4:3-5 KJV)

Wager and Greed

What drives us to do gambling? Is it about greed, or lack of materialistic possessions?

Billions of people all over the world are devoted to betting everything that they have with the hope of getting bigger things in return. Some are happy with the result, but many are shedding tears because of their fault.

Wealth gained dishonestly dwindles away,

but he who gathers by hand makes it grow.

(Proverbs 13:11 WEB)

We engage ourselves to gambling only for amusement; it is meant to entertain, but the thirst for something has always been in the heart of each and every one of us. As we lay our coins and silver on the table, our desire to gain more is becoming bigger. That's how covetousness starts to swallow us. It is like planting avarice, and watering hunger in our hearts.

We only want to make something in an easy way, or get back the wealth that we lost. A great number of tales were published on how people lost everything that they had because of the wager. While losing everything because of our naive behaviour, we unconsciously letting greed grow in our lives.

When acquisitiveness starts, we have to expect only harm. The love for money is spreading like an illness in our blood, and the thoughts to swindle people is coming to pass.

"No one can serve two masters, for either he will hate the one and love the other, or else he will be devoted to one and despise the other. You can't serve both God and Mammon.

(Matthew 6:24 WEB)

These kinds of vices broaden each day. We unknowingly commit the sin that can affect us and our family. We have to rationalise things on this earth, like how we think when we are doing works. Our eyes must always be open, and our minds must be clear to understand immoral things that are happening today. It only causes the fall and death of salvation.

[6] But godliness with contentment is great gain. [7] For we brought nothing into the world, and we certainly can't carry anything out. [8] But having food and clothing, we will be content with that. [9] But those who are determined to be rich fall into a temptation, a snare, and many foolish and harmful lusts, such as drown men in ruin and destruction. [10] For the love of money is root of all kinds of evil. Some have been led astray from the faith in their greed, and have pierced themselves through with many sorrows.

(1 Timothy. 6:6-10 WEB)

CHAPTER 6

SOCIAL MEDIA AND ITS HARM

Social media has become a necessity in our everyday life. We use our social media accounts to communicate with people easily. We always want to have the fastest connection so that we can do our tasks, and enjoy ourselves effectively at the same time. We can't deny that the rapid growth of technology, as well as the emergence of the internet, makes our life far easier than before. We have the power in our hands to do things right, or the other way around.

Aside from the fact that the 21st-century advances quickly, we also have to face the unrecognized truth about social media, and the harm that it causes the people, especially the young individuals.

Have you ever checked the social media accounts of your children, or your younger siblings? If not, then I advise you to investigate for your and their own sake.

I spend most of my time scrolling up and down through

my phone; I swipe left and right to see unusual things inside the internet world. It is common for me to see videos that amuse people, and showcase things that we can do on our own. Sadly, this kind of social site doesn't restrict young people to use their platform, but if they do, this young generation will still make their way to do what they want.

There are hundreds of million people who own accounts that are meant to harm a fragile human. They are hiding their faces, and attacking each other which leads to eradication. On top of that, unknown people continuously post indecent videos and pornographic materials. These kinds of shows slowly influence the minds of most innocent civilians, teaching them to be violent and aggressive. This eventually raises a defiler and debaucher person that is a threat to everyone.

Social forums of today are full of pornographic scenes and malicious shows that are publicised all over. Even the videos that they are making, which are supposed to be for entertainment, can cause distress.

Most of the time, we watch shows to pass the time of boredom, but we never look deeply at what we are actually watching. Thousands of movies, videos, and clips which support sexual immorality and unethical conduct such as adultery, gluttony, hatred, violence, rudeness, and lawlessness are spreading all over the world. We never take time to think properly and scrutinize these videos, and ponder on how they will affect our minds subconsciously.

But how and where are we going to start?

I will set no vile thing before my eyes. I hate the deeds of faithless men. They will not cling to me.

4 *A perverse heart will be far from me. I will have nothing to do with evil.*

(Psalm 101:3-4 WEB)

We need to accept the fact that the Devil uses everything to ruin us; he makes use of our company, and even the most despairing situation that we are into. So, what makes us think that this villainous spirit will not use social networking sites to impair our lives?

This kind of human creation promotes ungodly things.

We might not see it physically, but these tools are incessantly governing our intellectual capabilities. We have to start to straighten out our power of sight. Viewing not only the outside appearance of earthly things will provide you with some sort of certainty. Furthermore, let our minds and hearts work together to perceive that this mundane world is bound to bring not pain, but well-being.

What ungodly contrivances concealingly affect our spirits?

As I mentioned many times, social media and the one who uses it to promote harmful things to humans. I am not generalizing everyone, but most of the people inside the web are being used by Satan to do vacuous posts, information, clips, and images.

Predominantly, videos that aim to start loathing or odium are spread out like a plague. It lays the foundation of hatred between race, culture, and faith, and of conflict involving the outward forms people, and some other insignificant issues. These will develop violence and ruthlessness, that might end up losing a human life.

Ye that love the Lord, hate evil: he preserveth the souls of his saints; he delivereth them out of the hand of the wicked.

(Psalm 97:10 KJV)

Let those who love the LORD hate evil, for he guards the lives of his faithful ones and, delivers them from the hands of the wicked.

Aside from this, all of the uncouth and insolent topics that are revealed to everyone are the roots of the ill-mannered behaviours of mankind.

The ideology of being equal with everything and everyone has become more severe for the past years. We've been seeing all images and stories that are meant to mock God, as if we are one or equivalent to Him. For most teenagers, this kind of mockery of God such as fads, memes, and verbatim from the Holy Scriptures were created for amusement, and not for the intention of disrespecting the Lord. But what, actually, has been driving them to do such unmannerly interest?

Judgments are prepared for scorners, and stripes for the back of fools.

(Proverbs 19:29 KJV)

Be not deceived; God is not mocked: for whatsoever a man soweth, that shall he also reap.

(Galatians 6:7 KJV)

These kinds of people are clearly used by Satan; he desires to be just like God, and he is doing his best to influence others to mock and make fun of the Divine creator. For doing the things that we look at as an innocent act, but sin in the eyes of the Lord, we are making our way to the lake of fire.

That's what the Devil wants for us; he wants us to be by him, and suffer when the judgment day comes. The land of the dead is not ruled by Satan, instead, he will be tortured there, day and night.

In Psalm 139:7-8, it says that,

Where could I go from your Spirit?

Or where could I flee from your presence?

8 If I ascend up into heaven, you are there.

If I make my bed in Sheol,[a] behold, you are there!

God is the highest authority; thus, he can't be mocked. No one can ever be equal to him.

In addition to this evil dispensation, obscene acts and films are continuously playing not only for adults, but also for young ones. This form of amusement for adults are causing prurient curiosity to teenagers, children, and mentally incapacitated people.

All of the pornographic or explicit words, images, and videos that are published online are creating lecherous desire into the minds of humans.

How does this form immorality affect our lives?

It all started from looking and glaring at those sexual materials that are on TVs, social media, and books. Then, our minds slowly developed an urge for something; we eventually fell into the trap of thirst, then our bodies felt the craving and hunger.

We are adamant to try new things, and explore the flesh

that we desire. This leads us to becoming lustful for sexual conduct, and makes us behave in a lewd way.

If we're gonna read articles about the confessions of sexual molesters all over the world, we will, for sure, realise that every inhumane behaviour on earth started out from something.

They started from having an unusual desire that they wanted to do to a person. They wanted to imitate the offensive things that they watched to a human body in a venereal manner.

*25 But if the man finds the lady who is pledged to be married in the field, and the man forces her and lies with her, then only the man who lay with her shall die; **26** but to the lady you shall do nothing. There is in the lady no sin worthy of death; for as when a man rises against his neighbor and kills him, even so is this matter; 27 for he found her in the field, the pledged to be married lady cried, and there was no one to save her.*

(Deuteronomy 22:25-27 WEB)

Furthermore, this sensitive topic does not only produce

sexual violence, but also unfaithfulness.

Have you ever taken time to think about why some married couple fell into infidelity? Is it always because of unhappy union? Or, can it be because of seduction?

Almost every year, thousands of couples all over the world file for divorce. The most common reason is extramarital affairs. Some said that they were not joyful with their partnership, while others said that their minds were only corrupted that made them dive to immorality. Therefore, how many people commit adultery because of their concupiscence or strong sexual desire?

It is normal for a marriage to lose enthusiasm, especially, after staying in long years of partnership. The romantic relationship with our other half slowly fades as the years go by. In times like this, our wicked spirits can easily control our minds. Instead of working our marriages out, we are trying to look for our partners' mistakes and flaws. Then, we start to look at sexual things on the internet that can satisfy us.

16 *For all that is in the world, the lust of the flesh, the lust of the*

eyes, and the pride of life, isn't the Father's, but is the world's.

(1 John 2:16 WEB)

We are constantly looking and wishing for unimaginative sexual intercourse; our bodies yearn to try new things, but we know that our spouse will disagree with it. We can't accept our spouse's decision, and suddenly, we see ourselves thinking about someone else. By then, we are finally in a grave that Satan created for us.

We end up satisfying ourselves, while hurting our husbands and wives. Most of us forget to think about the life of other people involved in our marriage, like our children.

It started from innocently glaring; we might say to ourselves that looking or watching those objects of immorality will not harm nor influence us, but the truth is, no one knows when we will be tested.

19 Now the deeds of the flesh are obvious, which are: adultery, sexual immorality, uncleanness, lustfulness,

[20] idolatry, sorcery, hatred, strife, jealousies, outbursts of anger, rivalries, divisions, heresies,

[21] envy, murders, drunkenness, orgies, and things like these; of which I forewarn you, even as I also forewarned you, that those who practice such things will not inherit God's Kingdom.

(Galatians 5:19-21 WEB)

What really influences us to harm ourselves? Is it our own choice, or there's one particular thing that might affect our way of thinking?

In the last part of this chapter, I want to explain to you how media inflict self-harm in our lives. There are thousands of pieces of evidences that the internet is contributory in developing suicidal behaviour to a person. There are studies about how social media affect young generations when it comes to their mental health, such as anxiety, depression, bipolar disorder, and more. Almost half of the population who uses social platforms feels lonely, worthless, and pressured at the same time.

But how can media affect our minds?

Like I mentioned before, there are numerous people that

are creating accounts only to harm others. They are making horrifying graphic contents that subconsciously corrupt the minds of the young generation. Furthermore, cyberbullying is rampant nowadays; these delinquent human beings are concealing their faces to attack and destroy somebody else's life. They exist in the world of the internet to make someone feel unworthy and unloved.

On the other hand, social media also formulate pressure among people. Some diabolical influencers are setting an unreachable standard about how people should be. It can be a glamorous look, lavish lifestyle, higher position, and ideal circumstances in life. They want us to feel meritless; they want us to look at ourselves with no value. This darkness oppresses us to be perfect and flawless people that do not even exist.

While we are feeling the negative side effects of social networking sites because of all the wickedness created on earth, we are unknowingly hurting our embodiment. And every time that we are reaching for support, the Devil simply prevents us from getting one. It seems like he shuts everyone's ears to listen to our mourning. No one wants to listen, no one wants to help.

I am not saying that all people who committed suicide

are affected by the internet world; many of them lived with and suffered from psychiatric illnesses that lead to their tragic demise. In other words, there are suicidal people who were attacked by evil spirits, some endure disorder, and some are victims of devilish humans.

17 Don't be too wicked, neither be foolish. Why should you die before your time?

(Ecclesiastes 7:17 WEB)

CHAPTER 7

DEATH-DEALING IDOLATRY

What can people possibly do for their beloved superstars, or graven images? How far can they stay in admiring their Idols?

Living in the present-day generation, it is undeniable that people's creative mind is working. Futuristic performances of celebrities are all over the world; they are well known not only to adults but also to younger individuals. Avant-garde creations like music, movies, arts and crafts are truly mesmerising to everyone.

Before we go further, let's define first what idol and idolatry mean.

Idols can be people or things that are extremely loved and cherished by many. It could be objects that represent gods, thus, they are worshipped by people. Over and above that, idolatry is a greater or more severe admiration, reverence, and desire to someone or something. It is about worshipping people or things aside from God.

What do the Holy Scriptures say about idolatry?

15 The idols of the nations are silver and gold, the work of men's hands.

16 They have mouths, but they can't speak. They have eyes, but they can't see.

17 They have ears, but they can't hear, neither is there any breath in their mouths.

18 Those who make them will be like them, yes, everyone who trusts in them.

(Psalm 135:15-18 WEB)

It is clear that idol worshipping is a sin; we always think that idols only pertain to man-made statues, and are considered as gods. However, our extreme likeness to the people or things on earth is also an idolatrous behaviour.

What are the different kinds of Idolatry?

To make it easier for everyone, we are gonna divide this discussion on adoration into three kinds, including idolatry with false gods, profane, and religious or superstitious idolatry.

Idolatry with False God

Idolising a false god can cause serious harm to anyone. It leads to diversity and hatred amongst different religions because of the conflicting faith of one another. For Christians like us, we believe that there is only one and true God, but for hundreds of religions out there, they are convinced that there are more than one God.

We witnessed hundreds of events where people worship their statues made out of wood, gold, silver, and bronze. It is normal for us to encounter human beings that have contrasting belief from us. It is the actuality of life that we have to deal with.

On the contrary, a false god is not only the image, the carved wood or the non-existent gods; it also pertains to wicked spiritualities that wander everywhere. They are the hidden darkness within the cherished graven image.

*4 Therefore concerning the eating of things sacrificed to idols,
we know that no idol is anything in the world, and that there is
no other God but one. 5 For though there are things that are
called "gods", whether in the heavens or on earth; as there are
many "gods" and many "lords"; 6 yet to us there is one God,
the Father, of whom are all things, and we for Him; and one
Lord, Jesus Christ, through whom are all things, and we live
through him.*

(1 Corinthians 8:4-6 WEB)

Paul comprehensively said that there is only one and true God, but there are many divines and lords on earth. These gods are existing to manipulate people. They are scattered all over with their uncountable allies. It is not new to see people doing this act; we are living on earth where each one of us has a possibility to get deceived by these false gods.

Profane Idolatry

Aside from revering a false god, we are also in a deep hole of sin for idolising something that has no connection to sacred or godly beliefs. This kind of strong admiration or liking is not in connection with spiritual practices. This idolatry is practised not only by religious people, but also by someone who considers himself a non-religious being, or an atheist.

What does it mean?

It means that everyone is unknowingly worshipping entities that are completely different from God. They could be our favourite celebrities who can perform so well in front of the television. We adore these superstars so much that we don't even realise that we are already practising idolatry. We cry, we scream, we stumble, and we even pray for them sometimes.

I understand that we feel infatuated with these people. It is normal for people to be liking these performers, but what is unacceptable is for people to treat them as if they are equal to god. We shed more tears for them than for our saviour in heaven; some of us could have probably said out loud the names of our idols, but have not done the same for the name of the lord.

The young generation is so enthralled by these gorgeous and well-formed performers; they can sing, they can dance, and they have a sense of glamorous style. No doubt that even old people are captivated by their looks and talents. But how far can we go for this?

As I said, we are unaware of our behaviour. We don't know that we are worshipping these god-like creatures on earth, and we are putting our salvation in danger.

In addition to this, it is also possible to idolise the people that surround us; they can be our friends or our family. We always feel fondness towards them. We are pleased with their personalities, or positions in life, to the point that we want to be just like them. This, by all means, is also a form of idolatry.

[8] They that observe lying vanities forsake their own mercy.

(Jonah 2:8 WEB)

Every human walking with their feet on earth wants to feel good and look good. I see nothing wrong with this kind of desire, but what makes it erroneous is the uttermost aspiration of people for this, only for their outward appearance. It starts from an extreme wish of becoming the best, and the most prepossessing person amongst everyone; it is the urge that pushes us to look ourselves in the mirror, and flatter our own looks. We love ourselves so much, to the point that we are becoming unfavourable to others.

I am not against loving ourselves; I am happy to see other people having the confidence to walk and face the outside world without fear in their eyes. But what I am trying to say is loving our looks or our own selves too much can lead us to developing self-centred behaviour which may cause damage to people around us. We believe that we are superior to anybody else because we are the prettiest, the handsomest, or the most gorgeous. We look at others as ill-fated because they don't have the appearance that we have. We worship ourselves without even knowing it.

7 But the Lord said unto Samuel, Look not on his countenance, or on the height of his stature; because I have refused him: for the Lord seeth not as man seeth; for man looketh on the outward appearance, but the Lord looketh on the heart.

(1 Samuel 16:7 KJV)

After all of these, should we consider power and fame parts of wrongful admiration?

If we're gonna look back, and read the meaning of idolatry, it was stated that it is a reverence to or desire for something or someone. Moreover, if a person has strong desire, either for power or fame, he or she is undoubtedly practising idolatry as well.

People tend to idolise unseen things on earth. Fame is like glory, but not from the Lord, but from man. It is a human nature to seek validation from others; we are doing things that will please the public's eyes. The spectators will put us into the limelight- the notability that we want.

Once we reach the stars and the moon that we wish for from the world, we gradually feel the power inside our blood, running all over our bodies. The arrogance and pride swallow our minds, and all that we want is to keep our strength and prominence.

23 A man's pride shall bring him low: but honour shall uphold the humble in spirit.

(Proverbs 29:23 KJV)

Greed and love for materialistic things are growing and

continuously spreading inside us, corrupting our minds. The wealth and hunger for money are affecting our moral characteristics as humans created by God. These can cause destruction, not only to ourselves, but to people around us; we are harming them physically and emotionally. Corrupted people can take someone else's life for the treasure that they always want.

10 For the love of money is the root of all evil: which while some coveted after, they have erred from the faith, and pierced themselves through with many sorrows.

(1 Timothy 6:10 KJV)

For a long time, I can say to everyone that I had enough knowledge to see people through their eyes. I experienced spending my life with someone whose heart is full of avarice. His eagerness for money destroyed so much lives, and beautiful homes. He was never contented with having everything that most people want. His keen interest in money was a poison for him, and for the people around him.

I chose to separate my path from him, as the Holy Scriptures states in Psalm,

[1] Blessed is the man that walketh not in the counsel of the ungodly, nor standeth in the way of sinners, nor sitteth in the seat of the scornful.

Admiration for Superstition

[7] But refuse profane and old wives' fables, and exercise thyself rather unto godliness.

(1 Timothy 4:7 KJV)

Have you ever experienced walking into a home filled with traditions of men? How did it make you feel?

There are, probably, thousands of superstitious beliefs around the globe from different race, culture, and faith. We are oftentimes forced to believe on such things to give respect to others. It is more of a practice, ceremony or ritual that is performed by people for their deities. Some older people are doing the same pattern, not because of their god but because it was passed over by their dynasty.

For most people, following old beliefs will not cause us harm. Nothing's wrong with doing innocent things; however, we all know that it is more than that.

Practising these unprovable and mythical theories can be the source of our downfall. We cannot lie to ourselves that, not one day in our life, we believed in all of these. Most of us were raised in a family where superstitions are rich and vivid, and they are retained from generation to generation.

8 Be careful that you don't let anyone rob you through his philosophy and vain deceit, after the tradition of men, after the elements of the world, and not after Christ. 9 For in him all the fullness of the Deity dwells bodily, 10 and in him, you are made full, who is the head of all principality and power.

(Colossians 2:8-10 WEB)

There are quite a few unfounded beliefs from our childhood that we are still observing and performing until now, such as: preventing ourselves from breaking a mirror because it will bring 7 years of bad luck, prohibiting anyone to open an umbrella inside the house because it might cause a human life, tossing a grain of salt on one's shoulder for good luck, not stepping on a floor's crack for the reason that it would break your mothers back, believing that Friday the 13th is an unfortunate day for everyone, and more.

All of these beliefs are innocent as they sound; it might not cause a human life if we're gonna follow the path. However, are we going to risk our own souls and salvation for something that we never look upon?

Our parents could have introduced these tales and myths to our family. I cannot blame you if you are doing the same thing, but this book is written to show you that it is never too late to leave all our wrongdoings, and start a new life.

At the end of this chapter, I want you to understand that we never meant to disrespect you, neither your faith. We are writing for everyone who is willing to listen and acknowledge the darkness that is drowning each one of us, and embrace the fact that what is innocent for you may not be innocent for the Lord, and what is guiltless for you may be a sin for God.

25 For I don't desire you to be ignorant, brothers,[a] of this mystery, so that you won't be wise in your own conceits, that a partial hardening has happened to Israel, until the fullness of the Gentiles has come in,

(Romans 11:25 WEB)

CHAPTER 8

THE DEVILRY

As we grow older, we become more eager to try and explore new things. Our minds are full of imagination, and our hearts are filled with desire. It is human nature to think continuously, and dig into something unexplainable. We enjoy the feeling of excitement as our curious thoughts are wandering around.

Almost everyone has already heard the words witchcraft, sorcery, magic, fortune-telling, and more. We are amazed by the huge number of stories about people who witnessed and possessed such power. We start to think and question the legibility of these tales, wanting to see and experience them for ourselves. We want to be convinced without even thinking about the repercussion of our decision.

As we dig deeper on this subject matter, let me give you an elaborated definition and example of witchcraft, sorcery, magic, mediumship, fortune telling, as well as horoscopes.

Witchcraft

It is a religious practice of magical rituals of witches and wizards. Practitioners of this are believed to have supernatural powers and abilities, like casting spells and performing unbelievable skills. Also, they can allegedly control people or events.

Witches are known for making potions and holding spells for humans. Their powerful incantation can establish dominion over our minds, such as love spell, detrimental spell, and hypnosis.

When I was younger, I never believed in all of these. When people talked about witchcraft and the evilness behind it, my mind chose to brush it off and laugh. I thought that they were all old tales that were passed through generations. Maybe, I was too young and childish to visualise things. I never had the intellectual capability to see things from behind. For me, to see is to believe. I was conditioned to think that everything on tv was just products of the creative minds of the writers and director. They aim to give fun, and not harm.

But when I reached the stage of adulthood, I chose to investigate things on my own. I sought for guidance, not from a man, but from God. I prayed night and day for the Holy Spirit to give me wisdom. In the end, the truth was no longer concealed to me. I could finally see the gloom overshadowing the earth. My eyes are no longer shut; they are wide open to grasp the absence of light.

23 *For rebellion is as the sin of witchcraft, and stubbornness is as iniquity and idolatry. Because thou hast rejected the word of the Lord, he hath also rejected thee from being king.*

(1 Samuel 15:23 KJV)

Sorcery

Witchcraft and sorcery almost have the same meaning. Sorcerers use magical power to influence individuals. They are often associated with black magic. Many believe that sorcerers are using evil spirits to harm and govern humans to their destruction. One sample of sorcery is making someone severely ill for the rest of his life. Their victims may be a person whom they competed with, or an innocent individual whom they resent or envy. All these might sound like a myth; they are comparable to fairy tale stories which are meant for children. But the fact that all of these exist is something that we cannot leave alone.

In Malachi 3:5, it is written that,

5 And I will come near to you to judgment, and I will be a swift witness against the sorcerers, and against the adulterers, and against false swearers, and against those that oppress the hireling in his wages, the widow, and the fatherless, and that turn aside the stranger from his right, and fear not me, saith the Lord of hosts.

There is nothing new with this. Even during the time of Christ, sorcerers were all over. They are not for God; they are for the wicked ones.

Magic

Magic is the use of extraordinary means such as supernatural power and charms to manipulate a person, along with their beliefs, rituals, and behaviours. They believe that it is the art of using spells to control forces.

We commonly hear the term white and black magic. White magic is considered as good magic; it aims to achieve something pleasant. While black magic is regarded as bad magic, as its purpose is to only serve distress and injury to anyone.

At present, we primarily think of the word entertainment every time someone mentions the word "magic". It became part of our early years, until now. Television, book, comic strip, and more producers are constantly issuing amusing stories about this enchantment. In addition, we frequently hear children playing with their toys called magic wands and glamorous charms.

When watching films or reality shows on television, we repeatedly see people utilising their magical power to give relaxation to the viewers. They are practising stunts and unfathomable acts, like pulling a rabbit out of an empty hat, producing different kinds of things with their bare hands, making someone or something disappear in a blink of an eye, splitting the person body in half, and immeasurably more.

However, lots of us are convinced that this kind of supernatural doings are not only for amusement, but also for evil intentions, not for good ones. They say that white magic is pure and clean, since its purpose is to protect, bless or heal people from their illnesses- a selfless aspiration indeed. On the contrary, black magic is full of wickedness; its main objective is purely selfish and destructing. It is rich in performing malicious rituals to harm anyone physically, financially or emotionally. It causes no good, but torment.

[12] Stand now with thine enchantments, and with the multitude of thy sorceries, wherein thou hast laboured from thy youth; if so be thou shalt be able to profit, if so be thou mayest prevail.

(Isaiah 47:12 KJV)

Mediumship

It is the practice of mediating the connection between the living or breathing humans, and the soul of a deceased. The person involved is known as the spirit medium.

What is shocking for me, as a Christian, is seeing my fellow brothers and sisters in Christ acknowledging this kind of necromancy. One of my family members who goes to church every week is enthusiastically into this. I was in a state of disturbance when I heard her telling a story about a spirit medium and prognosticating. She is a devotee of a person who can talk to a dead soul; she can sit the whole day listening to the participants, and she is so convinced about all of the stories, guidance and suggestions that they are proclaiming. Then, I suddenly asked myself, "Do pastors in church never say anything about mediumism? Is it not written in the Bible that this evil spiritism is a sin in the eyes of the Lord?

Every time that I hear someone telling things about life and death communication, my whole embodiment trembles, the inner part of my body seems to be turning upside down, and I feel like my head is spinning rapidly.

Who won't be scared to a person who can talk to the dead?

9 When thou art come into the land which the Lord thy God giveth thee, thou shalt not learn to do after the abominations of those nations.

10 There shall not be found among you anyone that maketh his son or his daughter to pass through the fire, or that useth divination, or an observer of times, or an enchanter, or a witch.

[11] Or a charmer, or a consulter with familiar spirits, or a wizard, or a necromancer.

[12] For all that do these things are an abomination unto the Lord: and because of these abominations the Lord thy God doth drive them out from before thee.

(Deuteronomy 18:9-12 KJV)

Fortune telling

Fortune telling is forecasting or predicting future events. It is the practice of reading someone else's fate by using crystal ball, palms, tarot cards, tea leaves in a cup, pendulum, and more.

A huge number of people believe in all of these since the predictions appears to be so accurate to the lives of the patrons. The soothsayers claim to foresee the future; they use things to perform their duties, professing the future of their clients.

When I visited an Asian country many years ago, I was surprised to see fortune tellers outside an old church. Some people were just walking pass by them, while there are some who stopped for they were also curious about their future. I also saw individuals who came out from the church, sat in front of a table with tarot cards and crystal balls, and readied themselves to listen to the foretellers. Luckily, I didn't have the demon inside of me; I didn’t take a chance to sit and try. I only have one soul that I couldn't risk.

But where are these people getting their paranormal ability? In Ezekiel 13:23, it says that,

Therefore ye shall see no more vanity, nor divine divinations: for I will deliver my people out of your hand: and ye shall know that I am the Lord.

It is clearly written that fortune telling is not from our Lord God. We must stay away from acknowledging divination, instead, regard it as a continuous disease that may cause our lives. It is from the wicked, and not from the light. We cannot be naïve, and tell our selves that we don't know this evilness.

Believe that all of these exist, but never acknowledge it.

Horoscope

It is an astrological delineation representing the situation of the sun, moon, angles, and more. It is a forecast based on the position of stars and planets at a detailed point in time, or on somebody's birth date and year. It interprets character, personality, and upcoming events on the person's existence.

How many of you enjoyed reading your horoscopes that are printed in newspapers, or browsing the internet to know what is written for you?

Many of us were enthralled with this kind of prediction. We are reading these articles to know if they are accurate. We are comparing our situation to the conjecture published offline or online. We happily read and understand all the words regarding our personalities, traits, circumstances in life, and even the lucky numbers and colours for us. It gives the impression of being factual; it shows signs of actuality, and it appears to be true. Yet, all of these are not for God. Those who practice astromancy, as stated in the Holy Scriptures, will be put to shame. Doing horoscopes is something that should be banished and forbidden.

[19] And lest thou lift up thine eyes unto heaven, and when thou seest the sun, and the moon, and the stars, even all the host of heaven, shouldest be driven to worship them, and serve them, which the Lord thy God hath divided unto all nations under the whole heaven.

(Deuteronomy 4:19 KJV)

[3] And hath gone and served other gods, and worshipped them, either the sun, or moon, or any of the host of heaven, which I have not commanded;

(Deuteronomy 17:3 KJV)

In the verses stated above, it is comprehensible that the gleaming moon, millions of stars, and the shining sun are designed by the Divine Creator. He produced wonderful things for us. He established the world for humans who have dominion over the cattle, the wild animals, and the creeping things that crawl upon the earth. We have dominance over the fishes in the sea, and the birds in the air.

It is God who built everything for his beloved people. But why are they worshipping the sun in the sky? Why do they pray to the moon that our Lord just created? What happened to people's minds to depend their future to stars, and draw lines from above?

It is understandably stated that celestial bodies are not to be idolised. It is the Lord that we need to give reverence to. Still, we are imprisoned to the idea that we will not lose anything once we try. We are curious about everything, and we just want to explore hidden things on earth while being alive. But have we ever thought of the kind life waiting for us at the end?

The path where we should always walk on is becoming torturous; the long walk begins, and our feet start to slow down. Our light is gradually fading because of the sin that we choose not to know.

5 Trust in the Lord with all thine heart; and lean not unto thine own understanding.

6 In all thy ways acknowledge him, and he shall direct thy paths.

(Proverbs 3:5-6 KJV)

CHAPTER 9

WITHIN NETHERLAND

Have you ever heard the word cult or devil worship? What comes into your mind every time that you encounter these words?

We are living in a world where evilness is happening almost day and night; there are unknown societies that have been practising offerings, rituals, and far more. Diabolism is slowly becoming well-liked. As we can see, the Holy Scripture is not deceiving. Each word is constant, and coming to pass. It is terrifying to hear that the evil is wandering around. It gives us doubt about tomorrow, and a hundred questions of uneasiness in our mind. It creates uncertainty, not only for ourselves, but for God above. We are frightened about the bad things that can happen to us, or to our loved ones.

Each one of us seeks only harmlessness and security. We are not ready to face the underworld that will test our faith that we strengthened over time. Even though we have so many testimonies in life, we could still feel the anxiety within us.

Remember that the Lord gave us wisdom and power to see the colour of evil, and take a stand against unrighteousness, yet we are fearful.

13 For I the Lord thy God will hold thy right hand, saying unto thee, Fear not; I will help thee.

(Isaiah 41:13 KJV)

Every one should understand that demons are not the only spirit that can come right inside our body, nor phantom that can whisper on our ears. Satan uses ordinary people to spread out his wicked plan; sometimes, allies of darkness are concealing themselves to a fine and delicate man, or they can be a monstrous force that has been hiding in a seraphic face of a woman. They appear to be pure as the driven snow.

Frightfully, it will be hard for us to see people, in their realness, behind their smiles; devils are good at clothing themselves. It's their strategy to harm and influence people. Seeing them in the flesh of a human is just like looking for spirits in the air.

But what kind of evilness is making advances on us, and how are they performing their demonic plan?

[44] Ye are of your father the devil, and the lusts of your father ye will do. He was a murderer from the beginning, and abode not in the truth, because there is no truth in him. When he speaketh a lie, he speaketh of his own: for he is a liar, and the father of it.

(John 8:44 KJV)

It is common for people to watch scenes that portray rituals, offerings, and devil worshipping. For a young mind, it is only a fantasy written by a playwright, and put to life by the director. We often see movies showing harsh acts such as taking someone else's breath for their demonic practice; this shows that several people are praying more to Satan than to God. They are wholeheartedly admiring the devil in their front. Blood is used as a present, either a life of a child, or a life of a man.

It encourages young individuals to believe that being part of this immorality is something to be proud of. It is more of a statement that they are just like God, boasting about the power coming from the unholy one. They believe that the Lord exists, but the story in the Bible is the other way around. These people, who are half-witted, are convinced that Satan is righteous, and the villain is God.

Their words and behaviours are blasphemous; their actions are vile, and their outrageous faith can even cause life.

It might be new for you, but the world is full of secrets. The world is loaded with sins acquired by man. It offers lavish life, wealth, popularity, strength, and beauty. All of these are the desires of humans on earth. We want to have the best from this world. It makes us feel empowered, entitled and higher than others at the same time.

Now, I want you to close your eyes, and visualize this in your mind:

One day, your employer asked you to sit for a serious talk. He wanted to reward you for the hard work and great things that you have done for the company. As the conversation got deeper, he handed you over a piece of paper. He presented to you all the things that you want: cars, house, money and position. On the other hand, since nothing in this world is free, much more with material things, your superior asked for your life in exchange; you will be his slave until the day that you die. You will do whatever he says without complaint. You will be by his side either for good or bad, for heinous or pure.

You, then, silently questioned yourself, "Who wants to work for someone without freedom? But who can also deny such riches? Should I accept it or not?

You were so tempted to sign the agreement. Yet, there's something inside you, telling you that you deserve to choose, you deserve to be free, you have the privilege to do whatever you want. You were scared to be tied with a curse of a man.

Don't ever think that Satan only tempts humans as he once tried to entice Jesus Christ. In Matthew 4:1-11, it is revealed that the Devil allured Christ in many ways. As it is written,

4 Then was Jesus led up of the Spirit into the wilderness to be tempted of the devil.

2 And when he had fasted forty days and forty nights, he was

afterward an hungred.

3 *And when the tempter came to him, he said, If thou be the Son
of God, command that these stones be made bread.*

4 *But he answered and said, It is written, Man shall not live by
bread alone, but by every word that proceedeth out of the mouth
of God.*

5 *Then the devil taketh him up into the holy city, and setteth him
on a pinnacle of the temple,*

6 *And saith unto him, If thou be the Son of God, cast thyself
down: for it is written, He shall give his angels charge
concerning thee: and in their hands they shall bear thee up, lest
at any time thou dash thy foot against a stone.*

7 *Jesus said unto him, It is written again, Thou shalt not tempt
the Lord thy God.*

8 *Again, the devil taketh him up into an exceeding high
mountain, and sheweth him all the kingdoms of the world, and
the glory of them;*

9 *And saith unto him, All these things will I give thee, if thou wilt
fall down and worship me.*

10 Then saith Jesus unto him, Get thee hence, Satan: for it is written, Thou shalt worship the Lord thy God, and him only shalt thou serve.

11 Then the devil leaveth him, and, behold, angels came and ministered unto him.

Secret Societies and Their Practice

In Matthew 4:9-10, it is said that,

9 And saith unto him, All these things will I give thee, if thou wilt fall down and worship me.

10 Then saith Jesus unto him, Get thee hence, Satan: for it is written, Thou shalt worship the Lord thy God, and him only shalt thou serve.

As mentioned above, it is not hidden that Satan has the undue influence of corrupting the hearts of men by using the treasures of the earth; his objective is to spread his evil agenda.

The kingdom of darkness has been evolving throughout

time. It rapidly became favoured in the eyes of humans.

If we're gonna dig into the World Wide Web and the criminal cases in the occult, we will find lots of terrifying stories about these societies. It started from animal scarifies, up to human sacrifices. They are following their own rules which are written in their demonic scriptures. People are getting brutally murdered, children are losing their innocent lives, boys and girls are getting sexually assaulted, and blood is splattered all over during their worship services. Other than that, their symbols and signs are now trending, posted all over, playing inside our brains. These diabolical acts are serious threats to everyone, as they perform rituals that only causes harm.

Their Satanic law promotes sexual immorality, humanism, dark arts, and the quest of spilling blood- things that were prophesied before time.

37 Yea, they sacrificed their sons and their daughters unto devils,

38 And shed innocent blood, even the blood of their sons and of their daughters, whom they sacrificed unto the idols of Canaan: and the land was polluted with blood.

[39] Thus were they defiled with their own works, and went a whoring with their own inventions.

[40] Therefore was the wrath of the Lord kindled against his people, insomuch that he abhorred his own inheritance.

[41] And he gave them into the hand of the heathen, and they that hated them ruled over them.

(Psalm 106:37-41 KJV)

This group of evils is no longer in an impoverished and abandoned place as we see on television; they are well-funded organizations that have high standard places. Their members are finely dressed, and their technology is modern that fits the 21st Century. Moreover, their leaders have infiltrated security agencies to cover up their hideous crime.

Every time a person commits odious crime such as murder or sexual assault, he often tells tales about the group that he is into. He shares stories about his group that enforces life sacrifices in exchange for wealth and power. No matter how many people he killed, or women he raped, people will always believe that he is mentally unstable. He can be psychotic, schizophrenic or lunatic. With these, authorities usually fail to see the truth behind this kind of confession, and to listen to the reality beneath the horrifying crime; they will simply turn around, and fill their heads with comforting lies. People are wise about the affairs of man, but foolish with the acts of enemies.

Are Christians supposed to do nothing with all of these acts of darkness?

2 Again, thou shalt say to the children of Israel, Whosoever he be of the children of Israel, or of the strangers that sojourn in Israel, that giveth any of his seed unto Molech; he shall surely be put to death: the people of the land shall stone him with stones.

3 And I will set my face against that man, and will cut him off from among his people; because he hath given of his seed unto Molech, to defile my sanctuary, and to profane my holy name.

4 And if the people of the land do any ways hide their eyes from the man, when he giveth of his seed unto Molech, and kill him not:

5 Then I will set my face against that man, and against his family, and will cut him off, and all that go a whoring after him, to commit whoredom with Molech, from among their people.

(Leviticus 20:2-5 KJV)

We let the Bible answer our question. It is clearly said that whoever hides or closes his eyes while witnessing a man, immolating his own child, will be taken away from the Lord, including his family. It is the same thing in this modern age. We as children of God should never just sit, and do nothing, while others are occupied, doing unimaginable crimes.

Everyone must realize that we are not living on this earth only for ourselves; we are here to protect our fellow humans from falling into a trap. Individuals who use the earth that was created by God should at least help others from becoming soldiers of Satan because we will not have any difference from those who practised human sacrifice.

Christians of the 21st century can be better believers, not only inside the church, but also within their hearts.

And now it is time for you to ask yourself and embrace your response, "Will you be enticed by the wealth of this world offered by the evil, or you will keep your faith in God, and only for God?"

Should we sign with blood, or should we not?

CHAPTER 10

HISTORICAL CONVENTION

Traditions all over the world are truly fascinating. We are brought up in a way where certain days have to be celebrated. These traditions are detailed with history, beliefs, and culture. Although there are thousands of religions out there with contrasting rules and faith, acknowledging certain festivals such as Christmas, Halloween, Easter, and Valentine are regularly observed.

Christmas is scintillating- the colourful lights are attached to the walls, the bright colour of lanterns are hanged unto the ceilings, and the enormous tree is placed visibly in a noticeable space.

For some reasons, everyone loves Christmas; adults and children alike enjoy the joyous season. We love celebrating the special day with mouth-watering food and lovely music in the company of our beloved friends and family. Every year in the month of December, it is clear in our memories that our relatives are busy shopping, decorating, and planning the event, while we are sitting on a corner, eating sweets.

But before Christmas, another month being enjoyed by kids is the month of October. They called the celebration “All saint’s day”, also known as “Halloween”. This day is dedicated to remember the dead and the saints.

Most of the children today love Halloween; some are frightful, and some are not. They are knocking on doors for trick or treat, joining costume parties, lighting bonfires, and visiting a spooky tourist attraction.

Its traditional symbols are usually eerie like witches, skeletons, and other creepy things like jack-o-lantern which, perhaps, is the most popular one. This type of celebration is full of spine-chilling beliefs.

Aside from Christmas and Halloween, there is another tradition that most people recognize and celebrate. The Feast of Saint Valentine is usually celebrated by couples and elders who are in love. It is known as “Valentines Day”. During this season, stores are full of hearts, chocolates are popular and flowers are in demand; children also dress themselves as Cupid. It is, indeed, the day of showing deep affection.

In addition to all of these recognized special days is Easter, which is also very known worldwide. They often call it Resurrection Sunday. It is a Christian festival remembering the resurrection of our Lord, Jesus Christ. Many believers celebrate this day with special church services, candlelight, and meal with their families. The parents and elderlies hide candies and eggs for the children to search, and putting everything that they'll find into their egg baskets. They call it Easter Egg Hunt.

But what is written in the Holy Scriptures about these traditions?

8 Beware lest any man spoils you through philosophy and vain deceit, after the tradition of men, after the rudiments of the world, and not after Christ.

(Colossians 2:8 KJV)

The tradition of men is not for God; it is deceitful to many people, especially to young individuals. We are performing the traditions that are passed down by the previous generations. But what does God say about these cultural heritages?

Christmas

It might be a tough pill to swallow by many people but Christmas is rooted in idolatry. I am not gonna sugarcoat the fact that the belief that we are passing to our children is not pleasant in the sight of the Lord. It is blasphemy and unacceptable.

In Jeremiah 10:2-4, 8, it says that,

2 Thus saith the Lord, Learn not the way of the heathen, and be not dismayed at the signs of heaven; for the heathen are dismayed at them.

3 For the customs of the people are vain: for one cutteth a tree out of the forest, the work of the hands of the workman, with the axe.

4 They deck it with silver and with gold; they fasten it with nails and with hammers, that it move not.

It is easy to understand that God asks us not to follow the way of the heathen or the unbeliever. They will cut a tree out of the forest, decorate it with silver, as well as gold, and fasten it, standing, so it will not move. If we're gonna think deeply, we will realize that it describes the whole character of a Christmas tree.

This tree has been part of the said celebration. Everyone decorates it with bright ornaments such as crystal balls, stars, and shining ribbons. We are fixing it before the special day comes; everyone is placing their gifts under the tree, taking pictures with it, and posting them online, showing much love and affection. The lights amuse children; they are dancing and singing along with their blinking. Yet, all of these acts are not right.

What makes this tradition wrong?

It is because the tree that symbolizes Christmas is promoting idolatry. We are so fascinated with the idea that we are celebrating Jesus Christ's birth without thinking that we are idolizing, and admiring images created by the hands of man.

Also, everyone is excited about Father Christmas, known as Santa Claus, but we fail to remember the saviour of mankind,

Jesus Christ.

[2] I am the Lord thy God, which have brought thee out of the land of Egypt, out of the house of bondage.

[3] Thou shalt have no other gods before me.

[4] Thou shalt not make unto thee any graven image, or any likeness of any thing that is in heaven above, or that is in the earth beneath, or that is in the water under the earth.

(Exodus 20:2-4 KJV)

I understand that all we want is to please God; we want to celebrate the life of Jesus Christ. However, there are things that are sinful in front of the Divine Being. It may seem good for us, but unrighteous for Him.

Sadly, our ignorance is putting innocent children in danger. We make them believe that we are doing and giving all our efforts for God; their blameless characters are following our path. In 1 John 5:21, it states that,

[21] Little children, keep yourselves from idols. Amen.

Children should be protected from all ungodly acts, only the right lesson should be planted on their innocent minds.

Halloween

Halloween has no straight credit from the Bible. It is a western culture that spread out all over the world. It was derived from the pagan Samhain festival which is associated with human death. Ancient people were celebrating this day, believing that the dead would return to the earth.

Today, Halloween is observed with unusual costumes such as saints, witches, ghosts, skeletons and angels. Parties became popular for kids and teenagers; the day is full of fun, loaded with sweets, candies and entertainment.

The Holy Scripture, however, states, and we can it see for ourselves, that death is the end; only judgment is waiting for us after we lose our life on earth. There is no such thing as the dead returning to the world, as believed by the Samhain festival or Halloween.

27 And as it is appointed unto men once to die, but after this the judgment:

28 So Christ was once offered to bear the sins of many, and unto them that look for him shall he appear the second time without sin unto salvation.

(Hebrews 9:27-28 KJV)

I am gonna say this once again. Judgment is the only thing that is waiting for us after this life. We cannot pray to a phantom or communicate with it. Celebrating the spirits of the people who passed away, or saints who surrender their lives will not help us to gain our salvation. Christ sacrifices himself for humanity, and not for the dead.

5 For there is one God, and one mediator between God and men, the man Christ Jesus;

6 Who gave himself a ransom for all, to be testified in due time.

(1 Timothy 2:5-6 KJV)

This tradition can corrupt the minds of people; it can encourage evil rituals, divination, and occult practices that appear to be for amusement, and not for harm. Disguising as a witch or wizard, ghost, or any wicked creature is not for Christianity; actually, it is admiring darkness.

Should we celebrate the spirit of the dead or not?

11 And have no fellowship with the unfruitful works of darkness, but rather reprove them.

(Ephesians 5:11 KJV)

Easter Day

Before I start with this, I just wanted everyone to know that I am not trying to belittle the importance of Jesus Christ's resurrection, or to insult the beliefs of anyone. The objective of this written art is to show the misconception of the traditions that are being celebrated by my fellow brothers and sisters in Christ.

Easter was established from pagan tradition before the delivery of Jesus Christ. Babylonians and various groups of ancient people acknowledge this particular time as a holy day.

The term Easter was derived from the Anglo-Saxon goddess of spring and fertility, named Eostre. It also serves as a mythological creature, a rabbit, that laid eggs with different colours which symbolize life, fertility and birth. Most children are participating in a game called the Easter egg hunt. Aside from the non-religious traditions such as Easter eggs, the Easter bunny is also known in many households. These rabbits are known to deliver candies and chocolates to children who arrive in the Easter celebration.

However, all of these were rooted from non-Christian and pagan celebrations.

So, what did God say about Easter?

If we're gonna peruse the Holy Bible, we, for sure, will not see the word Easter, nor its corresponding words.

16 *All scripture is given by inspiration of God, and is profitable for doctrine, for reproof, for correction, for instruction in*

righteousness:

[17] That the man of God may be perfect, thoroughly furnished unto all good works.

(2 Timothy 3:16-17 KJV)

As expressed by the verses written above, all scriptures were given by our Lord God. All of the holy words are important for man's righteousness, and his good work. My question is, if Easter is important or does exist, then why is it not mentioned in the Bible? Furthermore, how many of you know the importance of being aware of the special day that we are celebrating?

[8] Howbeit then, when ye knew not God, ye did service unto them which by nature are no gods.

[9] But now, after that ye have known God, or rather are known of God, how turn ye again to the weak and beggarly elements, whereunto ye desire again to be in bondage?

[10] Ye observe days, and months, and times, and years.

[11] I am afraid of you, lest I have bestowed upon you labour in vain.

(Galatians 4:8-11 KJV)

Paul revealed that these Christians, who are drowning themselves in sin by observing all the special days, are hoping that they will become more justified and righteous as followers of Christ. False teachers are preaching wrong words, and they are using these people for their own eminence.

We don't want to disregard or ignore Christ's resurrection, but as Christians, we mustn't follow a tradition that comes from either darkness, or people's creative mind.

Valentine's Day

Valentines of today are highly commercialized. Millions of flowers and chocolates have been sold, as well as bears and cards that have been given away. Christians of today have split opinions about the celebration. Some said that it is totally fine to acknowledge Valentine, while some are not. The origin of this convention is unclear. Lots of articles claim that Valentine's Day is associated with Lupercalia, an annual pagan festival being held a long time ago in Rome every 15th day of February. However, Lupercalia is undoubtedly different from the celebration of Valentine's Day. This festival was vicious, and sexually explicit, and were practising animal sacrifices and rituals.

In addition to its origin, many people believe that Valentines is recognized for the remembrance of Saint Valentine, a martyr who died in Rome for turning down the offer of Emperor Claudius II. The emperor was said to be impressed by Valentine; he wanted him to be converted to Paganism, and be free from imprisonment. But instead of accepting the offer, Valentine tried to convert the emperor into Christianity, thus, he was sentenced to death.

Just like the others, if this tradition of man is truly beneficial in our lives and salvation, then why is it not mentioned anywhere in the Bible? Why did God warn us about this convention?

In Matthew 15:3, it is mentioned that,

> *3 But he answered and said unto them, Why do ye also transgress the commandment of God by your tradition?*

How long are we going to practice this belief? And when are we gonna stop corrupting the minds of innocent kids?

CHAPTER 11

FONDNESS FOR MYTHICAL CREATURE

Our childhood is filled with creativity; we love the colourful images in our minds, and the ideas behind them. Young and even old people admire mythical creatures. These mythological tales have been a huge part of everything in our life. They are usually utilized or mentioned in movies, books, music, symbols and posters. Also, rhey are vividly told and described in history. These stories may have come either from human's artistry or sometimes, reality.

Each of us probably watched hundreds of movies based on legends or magical beasts; we love reading books that are full of fantasy, and find mythical symbols and images modern and fashionable. In addition, some of us can willingly pay money for artistic body tattoos featuring dragons, vampires, and many more. Lots of businesses are also using these as themes. Indeed, mythical images are almost everywhere, and for everyone as they could be for children, men, and women.

Some of the famous mythical creatures that we commonly see on TVs and became part of our existence are vampires, fairies, dragons, mermaids, werewolves, unicorns, zombies, and many more. Children are fascinated with all of this. The little girls like to dress as if they are fairies, creep on the floor and pretend to be mermaids, and ride to the majestic unicorns that are in bright hues. Teenagers, on the other hand, admire television series and films with heroic and powerful werewolves; they can sit and watch for a long time, without blinking their eyes, as if they are one of them. They also love to watch thrilling zombie movies. The suspense and the edge of these give their young viewers some sort of exhilaration. Also, our parents are hooked with dragons, as well as their meanings. Dragon is one of the Chinese zodiac animals; it is associated with horoscopes that many people acknowledge until these days.

But are these myths for Christ?

Dragons

If we're gonna read the entire Bible, there are instances that the word 'dragon' is mentioned. The dragon represents the serpent which is actually the devil.

This evil creature tempted eve to eat the forbidden fruit. It persuaded Eve that she will not die, instead, gonna be like God, for her eyes will be opened, knowing both good and evil.

2 And the woman said unto the serpent, We may eat of the fruit of the trees of the garden:

3 But of the fruit of the tree which is in the midst of the garden, God hath said, Ye shall not eat of it, neither shall ye touch it, lest ye die.

4 And the serpent said unto the woman, Ye shall not surely die:

5 For God doth know that in the day ye eat thereof, then your eyes shall be opened, and ye shall be as gods, knowing good and evil.

(Genesis 3:2-5 KJV)

The Lord, as the Divine Creator, knew what happened for there's nothing that can be hidden away from him. He built the universe, and made man and woman. He has all the power to see things beyond. God punished Adam and Eve, placing them out of the garden of Eden, while He cursed the serpent to be crawling with his abdomen, and eating the dust of the earth all the days of his life.

[14] And the Lord God said unto the serpent, Because thou hast done this, thou art cursed above all cattle, and every beast of the field; upon thy belly shalt thou go, and dust shalt thou eat all the days of thy life:

[15] And I will put enmity between thee and the woman, and between thy seed and her seed; it shall bruise thy head, and thou shalt bruise his heel.

(Genesis 3:14-15 KJV)

The dragon is also mentioned in the book of Revelation. It pertains to Satan who wants to harm God's children. He is causing suffering and pain to everyone, deceiving people, and trying to conquer the world.

[2] And he laid hold on the dragon, that old serpent, which is the Devil, and Satan, and bound him a thousand years,

[3] And cast him into the bottomless pit, and shut him up, and set a seal upon him, that he should deceive the nations no more, till the thousand years should be fulfilled: and after that he must be loosed a little season.

(Revelation 20:2-3 KJV)

If it is written in the Bible that dragon is associated with serpent which is known for deceiving, then what makes us think that liking this creature is not a sin to the Lord? We thought that this symbol of Satan is appealing, putting it on our skin, printing it in our garments, and having it as decoration in our house, without us knowing that we are worshipping the darkness of the earth.

Unicorn

Save me from the lion's mouth: for thou hast heard me from the horns of the unicorns.

(Psalm 22:21 KJV)

[7] *And the unicorns shall come down with them, and the bullocks with the bulls; and their land shall be soaked with blood, and their dust made fat with fatness.*

(Isaiah 34:7 KJV)

Kids often think that a unicorn is a beautiful mythical horse, but the truth is, the Bible describes this creature as a real animal, and not a mystical character. A unicorn is a beast that has one horn known as rhinoceros unicornis. It is mentioned quite a few times in the Books of the Psalm, Deuteronomy, Job, and Isaiah. Its descriptions are far from the white and sweet horse with a rainbow-coloured tail; it is a wild and untrustworthy animal.

Will the unicorn be willing to serve thee, or abide by thy crib?

Canst thou bind the unicorn with his band in the furrow? or will he harrow the valleys after thee?

(Job 39:9 – 10 KJV)

The voice of the Lord breaketh the cedars; yea, the Lord breaketh the cedars of Lebanon. He maketh them also to skip like a calf; Lebanon and Sirion like a young unicorn

(Psalm 29:5 – 6 KJV)

I hope that one day, parents will be knowledgeable about the things they are introducing to their children. Our kids are innocent, and they don't have enough understanding about the evilness on earth. History changes reality into a fantasy for us to get deceived, and that's what exactly Satan wants for us.

Mermaids/Mermen

How many of us are so fascinated with mermaids or mermen? We probably watch movies, cartoons, and documentaries about these mythical beings, but still asking ourselves if they actually exist. The creature that has the head and body of a woman and legs like that of a fish is known as mermaid; her male equivalent, on the other hand, is called mermen.

This story has been living for centuries. Everyone thought that these half-human half-fish creatures are appealing in nature. Many believe that this story came from the Syrian goddess, Atargatis. She forbade people from eating fish. Ironically, when she died because of shame for accidentally killing her lover, her body transformed into a fish, but her head remains.

These creatures are, oftentimes, associated with storm, shipwrecks, and lots of tragic aquatic incidents.

On top of this, the Bible mentions nothing about mermaids or mermen, but the scriptures speak about Dagon, the head god of the Philistines. Dagon, a half man, half fish god, was believed to be the deity of grain and the harvest. His name is stated in the holy scriptures, but very seldom. It is written in one of the chapters of Samuel, mentioned in Judges 16:23 and 1 Chronicles 10:10, which states,

2 The Philistines took God's ark, and brought it into the house of
Dagon and set it by Dagon. 3 When the people of Ashdod arose

early on the next day, behold, Dagon had fallen on his face to the ground before Yahweh's ark. They took Dagon and set him in his place again. [4] When they arose early on the following morning, behold, Dagon had fallen on his face to the ground before Yahweh's ark; and the head of Dagon and both the palms of his hands were cut off on the threshold. Only Dagon's torso was intact. [5] Therefore neither the priests of Dagon nor any who come into Dagon's house step on the threshold of Dagon in Ashdod to this day.

(1 Samuel 5:2-5 WEB)

But do these verses prove the existence of mermaids or merman?

The answer is obviously no; they are not evidences of the legitimacy of this mythical beings. The Bible verses provided don't manifest the actuality, either a hint of reality, of the story of the half-fish half-human creature; in fact, it is only based on the human treacherous mind. Dagon didn't have life; he is made out of fallacy, merely a statue made by Philistines. He is the pagan deity that many people worshipped, believing that they would be blessed with their harvest.

As time goes by, people's imaginations become more

creative, turning fallacious narrative into child-friendly tales.

Admiring these kinds of stuff such as mermaid movies, toys for kids, decorations, and images are the same as worshipping false God.

Zombies

Before we start with this flesh-eating myth, let me define what is a zombie.

A zombie is a mythological corpse who is revived from death. It is said that this dead body is reanimated by using witchcraft or magic. They are speechless, yet walking dead men who are hungry for human flesh. The story about the living dead is common in horror movies and fictional works.

But do they actually exist?

The bible talks about the resurrection of Jesus, and his power to bring humans back to life. The scriptures mentioned three people who arose from death: Lazarus, the daughter of Jairus, and the son of a widow in Nain. All of these miracles were works of the Lord. However, it is never said that they became zombies; they were not wanting human flesh to eat, they were not wordless walking dead people, and they were really alive.

39 Jesus said, "Take away the stone."

Martha, the sister of him who was dead, said to him, "Lord, by this time there is a stench, for he has been dead four days."

40 Jesus said to her, "Didn't I tell you that if you believed, you would see God's glory?"

41 So they took away the stone from the place where the dead man was lying.[a] Jesus lifted up his eyes, and said, "Father, I thank you that you listened to me. 42 I know that you always listen to me, but because of the multitude standing around I said this, that they may believe that you sent me." 43 When he had said this, he cried with a loud voice, "Lazarus, come out!"

44 He who was dead came out, bound hand and foot with wrappings, and his face was wrapped around with a cloth.

Jesus said to them, "Free him, and let him go."

(John 11:39-44 WEB)

[23] When Jesus came into the ruler's house and saw the flute players and the crowd in noisy disorder, [24] he said to them, "Make room, because the girl isn't dead, but sleeping."

They were ridiculing him. [25] But when the crowd was sent out, he entered in, took her by the hand, and the girl arose. [26] The report of this went out into all that land.

(Matthew 9:23-26 WEB)

Apart from these, the dead will not come back to life anymore; they will rest in their grave, waiting for the final rule.

The only one who can do such a miracle is Christ. No sorcerer, witchcraft, magic or humans can do what God did. He will be the Judge of each one of us at the end, either we will have eternal life, or we will experience boundless punishment.

The verses provided below determine the reality of judgement day, and the second coming of our Lord Jesus Christ.

[5] The rest of the dead didn't live until the thousand years were finished. This is the first resurrection.

(Revelation 20:5 WEB)

[2] Many of those who sleep in the dust of the earth will awake, some to everlasting life, and some to shame and everlasting contempt.

(Daniel 12:2 WEB)

Vampires

Vampires and the rest of supernatural beings never existed or if they did, they were not for holiness, but for despair. Their monstrous characteristics have changed over time, and became enchanting to the ears and eyes of many.

Vampires are beastly humans with supernatural power. Their teeth are like sword, and their nails are sharp. They hide from the sun, and arise at night, wandering to consume blood from their prey.

Why is believing in vampires a sin?

[10] "'Any man of the house of Israel, or of the strangers who live as foreigners among them, who eats any kind of blood, I will set my face against that soul who eats blood, and will cut him off
from among his people. [11] For the life of the flesh is in the blood.

I have given it to you on the altar to make atonement for your souls; for it is the blood that makes atonement by reason of the life. [12] *Therefore I have said to the children of Israel, "No person among you may eat blood, nor may any stranger who lives as a foreigner among you eat blood."*

[13] *"'Whatever man there is of the children of Israel, or of the strangers who live as foreigners among them, who takes in hunting any animal or bird that may be eaten, he shall pour out its blood, and cover it with dust.* [14] *For as to the life of all flesh, its blood is with its life. Therefore I said to the children of Israel, "You shall not eat the blood of any kind of flesh; for the life of all flesh is its blood. Whoever eats it shall be cut off."*

(Leviticus 17:10-14 WEB)

Basically, blood represents life, a God-given gift. Eating, drinking or partaking in anything that is connected with blood is punishable; anyone engaged into this would face the consequences of his act.

Having an extreme admiration for blood-sucking vampires in movies or anywhere is a form of idolatry.

Werewolves

A werewolf is a person who can change into a wolf, and haunt people and animals at night, but remains a human in the morning. It is not mentioned in the Holy Words, but God warns us about fake teachers.

15 "Beware of false prophets, who come to you in sheep's clothing, but inwardly are ravening wolves.

(Matthew 7:15 WEB)

29 For I know that after my departure, vicious wolves will enter in among you, not sparing the flock.

(Acts 20:29 WEB)

During the era of Christ, wolf symbolises evil, or threat to God's children. Until today, wolves are considered dangerous to humans. However, werewolves are just imaginative tales.

Fairies

Fairies are imaginary supernatural beings that have magical power. They symbolise love and magic. However, the description of this creature is nowhere to be found in the Words of God. It might come from the story of a fallen angel who wants to deceive and harm humans. Fairies are associated with magic that is forbidden in the eyes of the lord. Thus, creations that have magic or represent magic is not from God, but from devils.

It is said that children are growing up with the belief that this tale has nothing to do with darkness. We, the parents, are doing our very best for our kids as we want them to experience an unforgettable childhood that they deserve. However, we also don't want them to be on the path of wrongdoings.

In Revelation 21:8, it is written that,

8 But for the cowardly, unbelieving, sinners, abominable, murderers, sexually immoral, sorcerers,[a] idolaters, and all liars, their part is in the lake that burns with fire and sulfur, which is the second death."

Magicians, witches and wizards, and sorcerers will face their second death in hell; they will be put into the lakes of fire. We must accept that it is a sin to believe in these fantasised creatures, as it is like believing in the evilness behind it.

In conclusion, it is clear that the demons are winning in deceiving us. They use everything, even the simplest thing, to corrupt our minds. We are so busy in this world that we fail to search for and investigate about amusing things that appeared to be so innocent, but naturally not.

No one is perfect or holy on this earth. However, there are a lot of people who are trying to be righteous, but unintentionally drown themselves in the sin that is unknown to them. I hope that, one day, we finally see the dark truth behind these fairy tales, and free ourselves from the curse that Satan set on us.

CHAPTER 12

TYRANTS OF THE WORLD

[13] Therefore subject yourselves to every ordinance of man for the Lord's sake: whether to the king, as supreme; [14] or to governors, as sent by him for vengeance on evildoers and for praise to those who do well. [15] For this is the will of God, that by well-doing you should put to silence the ignorance of foolish men: [16] as free, and not using your freedom for a cloak of wickedness, but as bondservants of God.

[17] Honor all men. Love the brotherhood. Fear God. Honor the king.

(1 Peter 2:13-17 WEB)

When I was in my teenage years, it was common for my mum to sit in front of the disciplinary office. I can't recount how many disastrous actions I did in school, but it is clear in my memory how I got punished for my terrible behaviour.

There was a time when I joined my friends to skip class.

We jumped over the wired fence, and ran. I enjoyed the whole day that I spent with them; we laughed, we drank, we smoked, and we did awful things that I can't even describe. When it was time to go home, I saw my mum standing in front of the door and asked me, “Where have you been?”

“School” I answered.

My mum disciplined me reasonably that day. I was shocked about how my mum learned all the things that I've been doing in school. I guess, it was still a mystery for me. Nonetheless, what is significant about that memory is how my mum reacted to my actions. I did something wrong, and I needed to face the consequences. She never raised her child with sweet words and sugar coatings; if I was not right, then she’d discipline me.

On the other hand, mum and dad are just like any other parents out there. For them, if you do great, then you will be rewarded.

I was a thick-headed kid. I can't say that my parents never talked to me about all the things that might harm me. They tried their best to protect me from the world, but it was difficult for them to defend me against myself. Sometimes, disciplinary action is the only procedure that a naughty kid needs; addressing things calmly is definitely not the answer.

I remember my mum and dad cried, and asked me, "What did we do wrong?"

From that time, I realised that everything that could make me happy in a very short time was not worthy. They were not even good enough to put my mom and dad in tears; it is all because of my rebelliousness, because of my naive acts.

Perhaps, you are asking yourself what is the connection of my story to this Chapter?

If we're gonna take time visualising our government, we will realise that it is the same with parenting. Our leaders are our parents, and the followers are the children.

A leader is someone who keeps our solidarity. When it comes to challenges, he keeps us, the body of the government, intact and united. If we did something erroneous, then we must accept the punishment. If we submit ourselves to the righteous authority, then surely, the penalty is not for us to take.

13 Let every soul be subject unto the higher powers. For there is
no power but of God: the powers that be are ordained of God.

2 Whosoever, therefore, resisteth the power, resisteth the
ordinance of God: and they that resist shall receive to
themselves damnation.

3 For rulers are not a terror to good works, but to the evil. Wilt
thou then not be afraid of the power? do that which is good, and
thou shalt have praise of the same:

4 For he is the minister of God to thee for good. But if thou do
that which is evil, be afraid; for he beareth not the sword in
vain: for he is the minister of God, a revenger to execute wrath
upon him that doeth evil.

5 Wherefore ye must need be subject, not only for wrath but also
for conscience sake.

6 For for this cause pay ye tribute also: for they are God's
ministers, attending continually upon this very thing.

7 Render therefore to all their dues: tribute to whom tribute is
due; custom to whom custom; fear to whom fear; honour to
whom honour.

(Roman 13:1-7 KJV)

But do we need to submit ourselves to the administration that shows no affinity and lack of excellence?

[4] Ah sinful nation, a people laden with iniquity, a seed of evildoers, children that are corrupters: they have forsaken the Lord, they have provoked the Holy One of Israel unto anger, they are gone away backward.

(Isaiah 1:4 KJV)

The most common problem of every governing administration is corruption. Most of the leaders of today think only of themselves. Their dishonesty is putting everyone in harm. They are making use of their power to do evil things to their people.

They steal billions of people's money, enrich themselves using the milk and honey of the land, and continuously extort whatever they want. They are planting shortage within the country, and in the end, the people are the ones to suffer. Some of these administrators are found guilty of countless immoral activities; some of the cases were disclosed, while numerous crimes are buried and never known.

Being corrupt is not a characteristic of a parent or a leader. They are not from God, but from evil. Their works are swallowed by darkness, their hearts are filled by wickedness, and their existence inside the government is a big threat.

I am not trying to oppose or go against any administration, nor saying that every ruler is unethical. I am writing this on behalf of everyone who can clearly see the unrighteousness that is happening in today's government.

Corruption is for the devil, and will not inflict any good.

12 And God looked upon the earth, and, behold, it was corrupt; for all flesh had corrupted his way upon the earth.

(Genesis 6:12 KJV)

What is the sign of lawlessness?

19 Thou shalt not wrest judgment; thou shalt not respect persons, neither take a gift: for a gift doth blind the eyes of the wise, and pervert the words of the righteous.

(Deuteronomy 16:19 KJV)

How many of you are regretful of giving an indecent return? It could be with a police officer, authorities, or anyone who is willing to offer their services just to make your life easier. I assume that you never understand that supporting their desire is an offence. I actually see no difference between the receiver and the giver of a bribe; both of them committed a crime which is punishable by the law.

Being part of such wickedness is a sin. We avoid choosing and taking the toughest route; instead, we consider playing a function that will cause severe avarice. Everyone wants the easy way in getting away from intricacies and troubles. For example, paying a traffic enforcer a small amount of money for over speeding, or gifting someone who is working in the municipality to help you get things done, without doing the proper procedure.

We are just as bad as them, and there's no excuse for these deeds.

Anyone who's on top should realise that God's guidance is one of the most precious gifts that he can have. The Lord will show him the way to success; he will be kept far from darkness, and his needs will be bestowed upon him. If the leader chooses what is right, then certainly, an incredible amount of wisdom, health, and materialistic things will be given unto him

15 He that walketh righteously, and speaketh uprightly; he that despiseth the gain of oppressions, that shaketh his hands from holding of bribes, that stoppeth his ears from hearing of blood, and shutteth his eyes from seeing evil;

16 He shall dwell on high: his place of defence shall be the munitions of rocks: bread shall be given him; his waters shall be sure.

(Isaiah 33:15-16 KJV)

Have you ever feel being oppressed by someone you know? How does oppression affect you as a human?

16 The prince that wanteth understanding is also a great

oppressor: but he that hateth covetousness shall prolong his days.

(Proverbs 28:16 KJV)

Every day, we never fail to sit in front of our television to see what is happening in the world. But not long after, we see ourselves reaching for the remote control to turn it off as we are getting so exhausted hearing the same news over and over again. Lots of countries in the world are being ruled by oppressive governments. The people of the county are rallying because of the unjust treatment they are getting. This prolonged cruelty is affecting the individuals who only want peace and equality. It causes mental health problems to many people, especially children who are too young to understand the occurrence of violence. Many of them died because of the riots and revolutions that rooted from selfish, oppressive and unethical administration.

The people who lead the nation fail to hear the mourning of their constituents. They undermine the needs of their countrymen which leads to violence. If the government is righteous, and the leadership is honourable, then the body of the state will be solidified. There's no way that people will cry and groan if everything is right. They will rejoice like children in times of victory, but they will behave like a wild bulls in periods of abuse.

14 In righteousness shalt thou be established: thou shalt be far from oppression; for thou shalt not fear: and from terror; for it shall not come near thee.

(Isaiah 54:14 KJV)

Can a nation be ruled by scurrilous and voracious men?

5 Let your conversation be without covetousness; and be content with such things as ye have: for he hath said, I will never leave thee, nor forsake thee.

(Hebrews 13:5 KJV)

I've been asking myself, so many times, about the origin of greed. I know that no one else is sin-free, aside from the

Lord, Jesus Christ, but I am aware that many people are trying to be righteous. Each one of us has desires in our hearts which are either abstract things such as power, fame, and love, or material things like money, house and more. But there are times that your ambition is becoming too deep. You start doing small crimes to get what you want, like telling lies that you have to say to get favours, and luckily, you get away with it. You eventually learn how to do massive violations because greed slowly grows in you. That's how greed starts. We are ignorant about our selves, and the desire that innocently sits in our hearts is unknowingly corrupting our minds. A man can never rule if he has an extreme desire for money, or even more. Great ruler thinks about the condition of others, and not of himself. Greed can slay, destroy, and damage, not only the people, but also their leader. Acquisitiveness is a threat; see it as a disease, and walk away from it.

18 And they lay wait for their own blood; they lurk privily for their own lives.

19 So are the ways of every one that is greedy of gain; which taketh away the life of the owners thereof.

(Proverbs 1:18-19 KJV)

Many of us have been played by a manipulative soul. We've been manipulated in school, in our workplace, and even at home. It takes so much time before we realise that we are being taken advantage of.

When our eyes are shut, yet physically open, we often look at the people around us as heaven-sent. We think that they are angels in disguise because of their flowery words and sweet gestures. But one day, our sight becomes clearer, and we see humans from beyond. They are conceited and only think highly of themselves. They are emotionally abusive, apathetic and wicked. We learn to step away from them; we don't want them to pollute our minds, so we walk to a new path.

[1] *This know also, that in the last days perilous times shall come.*

[2] *For men shall be lovers of their own selves, covetous, boasters, proud, blasphemers, disobedient to parents, unthankful, unholy,*

[3] *Without natural affection, trucebreakers, false accusers,*

incontinent, fierce, despisers of those that are good,

4 Traitors, heady, highminded, lovers of pleasures more than lovers of God;

5 Having a form of godliness, but denying the power thereof: from such turn away.

(2 Timothy 3:1-5 KJV)

If we want to avoid these kinds of danger in our lives, then it is rightful for us to choose not a manipulative leader, but a leader who honours his words, a leader who is not only good with speeches, but can rule the world, and a leader who do not have to conceal his true nature as he is really gentle and caring to everyone.

14 And no marvel; for Satan himself is transformed into an angel of light.

(2 Corinthians 11:14 KJV)

Should we comply with the authorities and the

government?

The answer is yes. God puts leaders to oversee us, and keep us united. Therefore, we have to respect their rules and regulations, and punish those who insult the laws and principles of the nation. Also, we should show appreciation of the service as they are doing their best for each and every one of us. If their works produce good fruits, then it must be celebrated, and they must be rewarded. No matter how great the leader is, if the body is a shame, then the country will still fall.

[3] Put them in mind to be subject to principalities and powers, to obey magistrates, to be ready to every good work,

(Titus 3:1 KJV)

Over and above that, we also have to judge the rulers using proper judgment. We must say what is not right, and reasonably ask for changes. We are not foolish enough to be introduced with a terrible constitution. We are humans, created by God, seeking only for peace and not war.

Everyone and everything on this earth need balance. If we disobey, then we must embrace the consequences as they will keep us grounded and disciplined. If the leader is immoral, then he must endure the punishment.

13 Submit yourselves to every ordinance of man for the Lord's sake: whether it be to the king, as supreme;

14 Or unto governors, as unto them that are sent by him for the punishment of evildoers, and for the praise of them that do well.

(1 Peter 2:13-14 KJV)

CHAPTER 13

RULER OF NEW ADMINISTRATION

It feels great every time that we hear good news on television. We are happy to see the economy slowly growing despite the uneasiness happening in our world. Many of us can overcome from the difficulties of life through helping each other; we usually witness the solidarity of people when everything seems to turn upside down.

We experienced natural disasters, violence, wars, and many more. In times like these, people are relying on their leaders. These leaders have the authority to govern the country for the betterment of everyone. We, on the other hand, are the ones who put our leader in his position through election.

When the time for choosing the next leader of the nation comes, we often feel hesitation in our hearts. It is an important role to fulfil, yet we are frightened that we might pick a wrong ruler who may put everyone in harm, instead of bringing them to a better life. There are times when we are so convinced by their sweet words and promises, to the point that we even forgot to know them from beyond.

The role of becoming a leader is fundamental for the organisation and unity of one another; so, it is important for us to elect someone who is willing to serve, and not to tear down the country. Someone who will put first the best interest of the people, instead of prioritizing his personal goals.

But more than these, what kind of ruler should we appoint?

Leaders Are not Self-Seeking but Considerate

3 doing nothing through rivalry or through conceit, but in humility, each counting others better than himself;

(Philippians 2:3 WEB)

Have you ever witnessed a team in a company, school, or church that is being ruled by a selfish leader? Did they achieve something great as a group, or they fail?

A ruler who thinks only of himself brings nothing but

destruction. His greed, either for wealth or position, is slowly poisoning his character which is supposed to be refined. When his personal interest is more valuable than the good of his people, then the nation will surely fall. A selfish man thinks about the power that he'll have once he takes the chair to command; his eyes will only see golds and diamonds, and his heart will be filled with a virulent desire. A true leader doesn't think so much of himself as his mind is set only for the good of everyone. It might be hard for us to see people who will put others first before their own needs, but this kind of ruler does exist. We must not let ourselves fall into the trap of heedless head; he will swindle the earth, and he'll run away, living us in agony.

[3] Let nothing be done through strife or vainglory; but in lowliness of mind let each esteem other better than themselves.

[4] Look not every man on his own things, but every man also on the things of others.

(Philippians 2:3-4 KJV)

Leaders Are Fair and Just

[14] The king that faithfully judgeth the poor, his throne shall be established for ever.

(Proverbs 29:14 KJV)

The 21st century is probably one of the controversial eras in history. The media are loaded with the latest propagandas, scandalous stories and unpleasant reports.

It becomes common to us to hear news with terrible headlines about the rulers of our country, such as dishonourable politicians, corrupt heads of departments, and vicious bureau chiefs. We watch hundreds of tales and documentaries about these kinds of people. Some of them are deceitful; they are stealing funds from various government departments, receiving bribes from private corporations for awarding tenders, and many more. Some of them are also connected to alleged violence, along with his people, and to a claimed inequitable justice system.

If that's the case, then why did we choose these kinds of people to rule us?

It is important and beneficial, not only for Christians, but also for each and every one of us, to select an honest and equitable person to rule over our nation, and lead us to greatness. This world is swallowed by prejudice against different races, classes, and religions, thus, our leader should know how to bring all of us together towards a common goal.

The scary part of living today is the fact that we might be judged in the ground of our ethnicity or status in life. There's a lot of horrifying stories that have been published all over the world about people getting unfair treatment from the government, especially in matters concerning justice. Men and women of different colour were killed, and never enjoyed their rights as humans, which, according to the law, is deserved by everybody. Asians, on the other hand, have a long list of complaints about the mockery and maltreatment that they've been experiencing, not only from the natives, but also from the leaders of the state where they are living. The whites, the considered minorities in Africa, are also being killed because of revenge which rooted from the racial discrimination that happened many years ago between the two races; whites, in history, have always been regarded as racist, egocentric and self-entitled race.

Lastly, the underprivileged people cannot even defend themselves from the heinous allegations that are sitting on their shoulders. This shows the great disparity between the rich and powerful, and the poor and helpless; the former has ways and means to cover and defend himself, while the latter is left with no other option but to embrace whatever the future holds for him.

But on top of all of these, I believe that if a leader will set an example to his people, then there will be a chance that these injustices, which are rampant and occurring for hundreds of years already, will be lessened, if not completely eradicated. If the ruler is fair and just, then everyone will get equal treatment.

4 The king by judgment establisheth the land: but he that receiveth gifts overthroweth it.

(Proverbs 29:4 KJV)

Leaders Stand Out

[2] I exhort therefore, that, first of all, supplications, prayers,
intercessions, and giving of thanks, be made for all men;

[2] For kings, and for all that are in authority; that we may lead a
quiet and peaceable life in all godliness and honesty.

(1 Timothy 2:1-2 KJV)

Everybody believes that great things will always shine like a bright star in the sky, the impressive work will surely catch the attention of many, and the magnificent invention will create exceptional power to help the land. It is the same thing when we have a great ruler. A leader is expected to always stand out amongst many because of his good work, moral character, and love for others.

A righteous man who is selected by people will be situated above to oversee everything with holiness and eminence. That is how the leader of today should be; not only good with words, but also with his work.

[21] Moreover thou shalt provide out of all the people able men,
such as fear God, men of truth, hating covetousness; and place
such over them, to be rulers of thousands, and rulers of

hundreds, rulers of fifties, and rulers of tens:

(Exodus 18:21 KJV)

Leaders Are Worth Following

[7] In all things shewing thyself a pattern of good works: in doctrine shewing uncorruptness, gravity, sincerity,

[8] Sound speech, that cannot be condemned; that he that is of the contrary part may be ashamed, having no evil thing to say of you.

(Titus 2:7-8 KJV)

How many of us used to be a follower of someone which led us to give our respect to them? It could be a celebrity, performer, influencer or politician.

A good chief will surely gain an enormous number of genuine supporters. He, who is known for having integrity and care for others, who is dedicated to and has love for his work and mission, and who can do wonderful works for his people, will surely be rewarded for the goodness and excellence that he exhibits.

It is like following influential faces in the world of internet, and watching shining stars on television. They get awards, become famous, and will always be remembered because of their brilliance to their craft.

When the righteous are in authority, the people rejoice: but when the wicked beareth rule, the people mourn.

(Proverbs 29:2 KJV)

Leaders Choose Their Battles

[31] Or what king, as he goes to encounter another king in war, will not sit down first and consider whether he is able with ten thousand to meet him who comes against him with twenty thousand?

(Luke 14:31 WEB)

What I observed about many people is their varying point of view about battles. Most of them believe that if you are standing for what is right, then you must contest, and fight for it. However, this way of thinking is not a sign of being a great ruler.

The leader will not put his followers in a situation that may destroy them. He will execute plan of actions, and will only aim for victory, and not for defeat. In the verse written above, it is understandable that the king's thoughtful consideration arose as he had doubts in facing a war with ten thousand men, against twenty thousand foes.

Rulers of today must know how to rationalise everything for the sake and success of their own people.

Leaders Are Willing to Serve, and Not to Be Served

42 Jesus summoned them, and said to them, "You know that they
who are recognized as rulers over the nations lord it over them,
and their great ones exercise authority over them. 43 But it shall
not be so among you, but whoever wants to become great among
you shall be your servant. 44 Whoever of you wants to become
first among you, shall be bondservant of all. 45 For the Son of
Man also came not to be served, but to serve, and to give his life
as a ransom for many."

(Mark 10:42-45 WEB)

We know that heads of today need to be protected, such as the president, politicians, civil servants and heads of departments. Their safety and security are the topmost concerns of everyone. Lots of opposing parties want to turn them down, as the power that they have to govern the nation is a dream of many, if these people will have the position that everyone desires, it will be easy for them to do all the things they want for themselves. A great and true leader is willing to work for his countrymen, and doesn't think highly of himself. He serves the nation with his good heart, and doesn't need to be served by everyone.

Leaders Are strong

[7] For the overseer must be blameless, as God's steward, not self-pleasing, not easily angered, not given to wine, not violent, not greedy for dishonest gain; [8] but given to hospitality, a lover of good, sober minded, fair, holy, self-controlled, [9] holding to the faithful word which is according to the teaching, that he may be

able to exhort in the sound doctrine, and to convict those who contradict him.

[10] For there are also many unruly men, vain talkers and deceivers, especially those of the circumcision, [11] whose mouths must be stopped: men who overthrow whole houses, teaching things which they ought not, for dishonest gain's sake. [12] One of them, a prophet of their own, said, "Cretans are always liars, evil beasts, and idle gluttons." [13] This testimony is true. For this cause, reprove them sharply, that they may be sound in the faith, [14] not paying attention to Jewish fables and commandments of men who turn away from the truth.

(Titus 1:7-14 WEB)

Are we going to appoint someone who is half-hearted and frail? Are we going to take a chance on a man who is not tough to handle difficult and sensitive matters? Will the nation be firm and strong if the head, himself, is not?

These questions are significant, not only for an individual but for everyone, especially when the period for choosing our leader comes. A man who has the wisdom to plan great things is nothing if he is not strong enough to implement it. A leader who gets discouraged easily is weak, and may pull everyone down to the ground; this might require years for a nation to stand again from this downfall. The strong ruler, on the contrary, is competent.

His objective is greatness, and his indestructible power will put his nation on top of the world.

Leaders Are Great Planners and Intelligent Thinkers

3 For I say through the grace that was given me, to every man who is among you, not to think of himself more highly than he ought to think; but to think reasonably, as God has apportioned to each person a measure of faith. 4 For even as we have many members in one body, and all the members don't have the same function, 5 so we, who are many, are one body in Christ, and individually members of one another,

6 having gifts differing according to the grace that was given to us: if prophecy, let's prophesy according to the proportion of our faith; 7 or service, let's give ourselves to service; or he who teaches, to his teaching; 8 or he who exhorts, to his exhorting; he who gives, let him do it with generosity; he who rules, with diligence; he who shows mercy, with cheerfulness.

(Romans 12:3-8 WEB)

Great rulers of the past showed efficiency in implementing the mandates set by the people, for the people. A man is judged by the fruits of his labour, and the interests of his heart. A good leader listens to a wise council around him, fulfilling important positions. He, and everyone that surrounds him are wise, and they are capitalizing on this trait in doing worthwhile and purpose-driven tasks, and not in executing corrupt and selfish things. They are knowledgeable in planning and doing programs that may be beneficial to everyone. The one who leads the nation can do many things; he is talented and sharp to oversee things with respect and dignity.

An intelligent person executes great intentions. Being strong and caring will not be enough for the greatness of the nation. It is important to always regard that in governing, the mind should be allowed to lead, and the heart will just follow.

2 The overseer therefore must be without reproach, the husband
of one wife, temperate, sensible, modest, hospitable, good at
teaching; 3 not a drinker, not violent, not greedy for money, but
gentle, not quarrelsome, not covetous; 4 one who rules his own
house well, having children in subjection with all
reverence; 5 (but how could someone who doesn't know how to
rule one's own house take care of God's assembly?) 6 not a new
convert, lest being puffed up he fall into the same condemnation
as the devil. 7 Moreover he must have good testimony from those
who are outside, to avoid falling into reproach and the snare of

the devil.

(1 Timothy 3:2-7 WEB)

But are we actually doing our job in selecting a ruler who will oversee us?

While the children of Christ are lying in deep sleep, the kingdom of darkness is strategically making advances by filling crucial positions in power, in the private and government sector, with bad leaders. While it is true that we doing our very best to be righteous in the eyes of the Lord, but it slipped in our minds that we also need to think about our fellows. Are they fine? Are they surviving? Are they keeping their body and soul together? We know that we cannot help each and every living soul on earth, but by choosing a leader that will help and nurture our nation, magnificent things will surely be achieved.

The reason why most administrations are turning upside down is because Christians are already caught up with their own lives. Also, it is a fact that these observations are not only happening inside the government, but also to thousands of companies, industries, and even churches all over the world.

I pray that one day, we will be ruled by great leaders, so we, the followers, and this nation, in general, will finally rejoice.

CHAPTER 14

WORLD'S DIFFICULTIES

What comes into your mind every time that you hear about world's problems? Is it only about the economic condition or status of the country? Is it about the unemployment rate and poverty level?

In this chapter, I will mention problems of the world that has been accumulated for thousands of years.

World War

[2] I will stir up the Egyptians against the Egyptians, and they will fight everyone against his brother, and everyone against his neighbor; city against city, and kingdom against kingdom. (Isaiah 19:2 WEB)

A decade ago, I can still remember that particular day when I woke up to go to work; I made a cup of tea for myself, and opened the television. It was a fine day for me. I could still hear the birds chirping, and feel the fresh air coming through my window. The news was relaxing, until I decided to look for other reports to watch; in an instant, everything about that day changed.

People were grieving all over, the vast ground was covered with blood, and lifeless bodies were all around.

I could feel the bullets that perched deep into the bodies. The skins were burnt by the fire of hell, and the fleshes were falling off the bone. There was a conflict between countries; the cry of innocent people could be heard, and everyone was scared at that moment. The video from the TV troubled my mind, and I asked myself, "What if it happened right here? Am I gonna survive?"

I remembered closing my eyes, and started to call the name of the Lord. I realised how fortunate I was for having a life that was far from violence. I prayed to thank God for all the miracles that he gave upon my life, and requested serenity between and among different nations.

Then I woke up from a deep sleep; I felt glad that it was just a dream.

Every time that I am listening about the things on earth, I am getting more dismayed. Many innocent lives were sacrificed and have suffered because of the war that man cultivated.

Have we not seen the mourning of a mother while looking at her lifeless husband? Did we even feel sorry to the victims of war, and sympathize to their family as they gaze, while weeping, at their lifeless member? Is it completely fine with us witnessing all of these?

Country against another country is causing only harm, and nothing else. Influential people that hold positions and power manipulate things to incite battle for their avarice.

Fortunately, some people all over the world are strong and inspiring enough to use social media platforms to support one another. These people aim to promote peace and security for the innocents. We might not stop the conflict, but we can start to help each other, and do something to lessen the impact of it to each of us.

But will these oppressors stop? Won't they heed to the groans and moans of men?

He made many stumble. Yes, they fell on one another.

They said, 'Arise! Let's go again to our own people, and to the land of our birth, from the oppressing sword.'

(Jeremiah 46:16 WEB)

Diseases

[19] He is chastened also with pain on his bed, With continual strife in his bones;

[20] So that his life abhors bread, And his soul dainty food.

[21] His flesh is so consumed away, that it can't be seen; His bones that were not seen stick out.

[22] Yes, his soul draws near to the pit, And his life to the destroyers.

[23] "If there is beside him an angel, An interpreter, one among a thousand, To show to man what is right for him;

[24] Then God is gracious to him, and says, 'Deliver him from going down to the pit, I have found a ransom.'

[25] His flesh shall be fresher than a child's; He returns to the days of his youth.

[26] He prays to God, and he is favorable to him, So that he sees his face with joy: He restores to man his righteousness.

[27] He sings before men, and says, 'I have sinned, and perverted that which was right, And it didn't profit me.

[28] He has redeemed my soul from going into the pit, My life shall see the light.'

[29] "Behold, God works all these things, Twice, yes three times, with a man,

(Job 33:19-29 WEB)

If we're gonna read articles, books, and even news, we will find out that there are approximately a thousand diseases out there. Some have cures, while some don't have. All of us are scared to let go of the life that God gave us, but on the contrary, we are irresponsible to our own bodies. For an instance, drinking water is probably the easiest thing to do on earth, but we failed and continuously failing to do it. In the end, we are suffering from diseases such as Urinary Tract Infection, kidney problems, skin diseases and many more.

I am not saying that these health problems are because of our reckless lifestyle. In fact, it can be rooted from our genes, transmission of infectious agents, or tragedy.

When I was young, I remembered my dad crying because of the tragic death of his sister. His eyes were filled with grief. At the age of thirty-four, my aunt died because of a heart attack. My family was shattered, and the sorrow slowly swallowed the family that once was full of happiness. We couldn't believe with the cause of my aunt's death, but that was the reality. Heart ailment is one of the deadliest diseases, even up to now. No matter how young you are, if it's in your fate to have a serious health condition, then you cannot do anything to change it. The only thing that you can do is to help yourself by doing what is right for you.

Is it your fault to be born with diabetes or skin diseases? The simple answer is certainly no. it is not your mistake, nor your failure. However, you can do something about it. Science developed remedies to ease the sufferings of people.

The intelligent mind of a man wildly helps the lives of sick and ailing people for thousands of years now. Scientists developed medicines, tools, equipment, and procedures for specific needs of ill people.

In addition, we all know that not only science can help us. Remember what happened to Job?

Satan took his animals, servants, and children, and afflicted him with sores, but he never denounced God which

Satan actually wanted. His wife wanted him to curse God, but he refused. His friends thought that Job and God were not good, but instead of getting furious, he prayed for his friends, and God heard his prayer. The Lord blessed him abundantly, and He gave Job more than what he had before because he didn't curse God.

We can pray for the things that seem to be falling apart. We might think that our illness is already the end, but nothing is impossible to our Lord who gave life to us. Miraculous things can happen when we begged for it from Him.

19 And it came to pass, that in process of time, after the end of two years, his bowels fell out by reason of his sickness: so he died of sore diseases. And his people made no burning for him, like the burning of his fathers.

(2 Chronicles 21:19 KJV)

Stumbling Block in Nourishment

2 Wherefore do ye spend money for that which is not bread? and your labour for that which satisfieth not? hearken diligently unto me, and eat ye that which is good, and let your soul delight itself in fatness.

(Isaiah 55:2 KJV)

Food is one of the necessities in a man's life. We get from them the energy that we need to perform our daily tasks, and improve our well-being. We are eating because we need to. All of us always want to be healthy, and we also pray for our wellness. However, the food that we like to consume can bring, not vitality, but harm.

I can't remember myself praying when I'm eating junk foods. It might sound odd but It only takes a little bit of common sense to understand what I said. We are praying to thank the Lord for providing us with healthy food, and for blessing us with good health and nourishment. But are frozen pizza, chips, candies, sodas and junk foods counted?

How can we thank God for the food that causes damage to our bodies?

12 in which were all kinds of four-footed animals of the earth, wild animals, reptiles, and birds of the sky. 13 A voice came to him, "Rise, Peter, kill and eat!"

14 But Peter said, "Not so, Lord; for I have never eaten anything that is common or unclean."

[15] A voice came to him again the second time, "What God has cleansed, you must not call unclean."

(Acts 10:12-15 WEB)

In the verses stated above, it is pretty clear that what God has made for us to eat is clean. Our Lord never wanted to hurt us in any way, even with the things that we eat. He made everything clean for his people to consume.

On the other hand, food that has been genetically modified, polluted with pesticides, processed with preservatives, and mixed with artificial flavours such as sodas, candies, frozen goods, and pre-packed meals and chips, also known as crisps, are not made by God. All of these are man-made or lab-made food that might cause harm to our bodies.

Do you think God will listen to us if we are not even listening to him?

Pollution

[7] I brought you into a plentiful land

to eat its fruit and its goodness;

but when you entered, you defiled my land,

and made my heritage an abomination.

(Jeremiah 2:7 WEB)

Many decades ago, it was still clear in my memory the beauty of my homeland. It was clean, pristine and the air is unmistakably fresh and unpolluted. But years went by, and the place that was once clear is now polluted.

The greens and soil that have been the source of good fruits and oxygen are nowhere to be seen. They are now replaced by buildings that secrete wastes which destroy the beauty of the earth.

The trees that once gave us fresh air were turned into planks of woods which will be used in developing infrastructures. The smell of the place is now stinky and awful, the view is outrageous, and even the waters are no longer clear blue. Garbage are scattered all over, and the water is murky. Unpleasant, not magnificent, is the rightful description for the place where I was raised.

It is the fact that we can't get enough. People are continuously doing what they want, and they are not even thinking and realising that the earth that was created for us to live in is slowly getting damaged. They only think about how they can profit or make money out of our natural resources. Also, most of us are so foolish to recklessly dump their rubbish anywhere, as if they don't know where such trashes are supposed to be thrown. It seems so natural for them to act that way, as if there's no law enacted on such violation.

God is truly not happy with the ways of man. We only want to live for ourselves, and refuse to function as rulers of the land.

5 The earth also is defiled under the inhabitants thereof; because they have transgressed the laws, changed the ordinance, broken the everlasting covenant.

(Isaiah 24:5 KJV)

Overcoming Our Worries

[33] I have told you these things, that in me you may have peace. In the world you have trouble; but cheer up! I have overcome the world."

(John 16:33 WEB)

Is there no way that we can break out from all these problems?

We might feel hopeless and unfortunate about what's going on, but we must understand that we can't rely completely on a man. Our understanding is not enough to relieve us from all these difficulties. There will always be a time that we will need God in our lives. We must pray with all our hearts, not only for our sake, but for everyone, no matter what race, country, or faith.

Pray for those who are sick, and help those who are needy.

Soon, our unity will overpower the darkness, and tranquility will be ours to enjoy and keep. All we need is to submit ourselves to the Lord, and believe that He will always lead us on a path where there's no harm.

5 Trust in the Lord with all thine heart; and lean not unto thine own understanding.

6 In all thy ways acknowledge him, and he shall direct thy paths.

(Proverbs 3:5-6 KJV)

CHAPTER 15

IT WILL NEVER BE TOO LATE

[9] But as it is written,
"Things which an eye didn't see, and an ear didn't hear, which didn't enter into the heart of man, these God has prepared for those who love him."
(1 Corinthians 2:9 WEB)

Who among us believe in hell? And who among us want to go to heaven?

I'm sure that you probably know the answer to these questions. Most of us believe in the existence of paradise that God created for His people, and no one wants to be in a place where there's only torment and agony. We are continuously believing on the things that we can't hear or even see; we have faith in something that is invisible.

However, is believing enough to see the kingdom of God?

We might say to ourselves that knowing God is acceptable, but the truth is, it is not enough. Yes, we acknowledge the presence of the Divine Creator, but we all know that it is not the only thing that we should do. We have to fulfil our role as Christians, and we need to do what is righteous in the eyes of our Lord.

Some might ask, "Isn't it that heaven is just an imagination?"

In revelation 21:1-5, it says that,

[1] I saw a new heaven and a new earth: for the first heaven and the first earth have passed away, and the sea is no more. [2] I saw the holy city, New Jerusalem, coming down out of heaven from God, prepared like a bride adorned for her husband. [3] I heard a loud voice out of heaven saying, "Behold, God's dwelling is with people, and he will dwell with them, and they will be his people, and God himself will be with them as their God. [4] He will wipe away every tear from their eyes. Death will be no more; neither will there be mourning, nor crying, nor pain, any more. The first things have passed away." [5] He who sits on the throne said, "Behold, I am making all things new." He said, "Write, for these words of God are faithful and true."

(Revelation 21:1-5 WEB)

Heaven is the place where we can find our much-desired peace. That is what all of us yearn- to be in a place where we will hear no mourn and cry, a kingdom of happiness and not pain. This paradise is not just an imagination, but a real one.

Each day, we close our eyes, and thank God for the life that He gave us. We are happy to get up knowing that we can still face the world even if it's difficult. We are smiling as we wake up from our beds, and do our best to compete with the struggles that life throws on us. We are indeed fighters; however, our strengths and moral beliefs have limitations. I agree that we can do good things, but all of us can be caught up in this world.

We are trying to be better individuals every day, but we fail to do so. Our morality is getting tested at work, home, almost everywhere. We are tempted to do disastrous things because we are only humans; we make mistakes, and we are not holy. Our hearts yearn for more worldly things, to the point that we are motivated or forced to do wicked deeds.

For there is no good tree that produces rotten fruit; nor again a rotten tree that produces good fruit. [44] For each tree is known by its own fruit. For people don't gather figs from thorns, nor do they gather grapes from a bramble bush. [45] The good man out of the good treasure of his heart brings out that which is good, and the evil man out of the evil treasure of his heart brings out that which is evil, for out of the abundance of the heart, his mouth speaks.

(Luke 6:43-45 WEB)

The evilness within our souls is growing, and we are gradually bringing out the worst piece of us. The alarming part is that people will see us like a noxious matter that bring no good to anyone, like an awful tree that will not produce good fruit.

We often hear people saying that they have good hearts, and believe that they will inherit the kingdom of God although they have sinned Him for not doing what is written in the Bible.

One should be cautious about this perception, as it is written in Jeremiah 17:9,

The heart is deceitful above all things and it is exceedingly corrupt.

Who can know it?

Our hearts yearn for things that can be harmful to us. It could be lustful objects, materialistic things, or anything wicked; they are also deceitful and quick to judge. We are greedy, as we want to get things in any way possible, evil route or not.

We must always remember that our Creator will never give a gift that is not good. He will bless us with things that we pray for, but the cravings that come from our hearts are definitely not from him. His presents are perfect and promising, but we fail to see it because we are busy with things that we desire on earth.

17 Every good gift and every perfect gift is from above, coming down from the Father of lights, with whom can be no variation, nor turning shadow.

(James 1:17 WEB)

As I said, we wanted to live in a kingdom that emulates God's glory; a place that is full of happiness and love. But can we declare to ourselves that we deserve to be in the holy place?

No one can say who's going to heaven, and who's not; only the Lord, Jesus Christ can. God will call the those who did what He commanded, and he will not allow those who chose the way against righteousness.

For our of the heart come evil thought, murders, adulteries, sexual sins, thefts, false testimony, and blasphemies.

(Matthew 15:19 WEB)

Is it too late for someone who sinned God?

For all the things that we have done, as I mentioned from the previous chapters of this book, God will always be loving, He never wanted harm, but everlasting life, to everyone. He never wished destruction for His people, but repentance from them. It is not too late to be on God's side. He will guide us in a way that we will never get hurt. In Psalm 32:8, it is clearly written that,

I will instruct you and teach you in the way which you shall go. I will counsel you with my eye on you.

We might have committed sins in the past, but He never closed His heart for us. God is patiently waiting for His children.

I cannot provide an answer to your question if you have a room in God's kingdom, but one thing is for sure, if you are willing to change now for your salvation, then God will certainly not be letting you down.

[9] The Lord is not slow concerning his promise, as some count slowness; but he is patient with us, not wishing that anyone should perish, but that all should come to repentance.

(2 Peter 3:9 WEB)

One day, at your life's last minute, I pray that you will no longer be asking yourself about which entrance are you going to walk on, for the reason that you want to be different, I hope that you will choose to be a better Christian, and leave your immorality behind. And for that, you will surely be favoured by God.

As your brother in Christ I want to ask you a question: do you think you have a place in heaven?

[5] Jesus answered, "Most certainly I tell you, unless one is born of water and spirit, he can't enter into God's Kingdom. [6] That which is born of the flesh is flesh. That which is born of the Spirit is spirit. (John 3:5-6 WEB)

ABOUT THE AUTHOR

Keegan Naidoo is one of the well-praised wealth managers in one of the biggest banks in South Africa way back in 2014, investing close to billion Rands of people's money. However, he was diagnosed with anxiety and severe depression that affected his relationship with other people. He was battling with his physical disability since that same year, making it difficult for him to move for eight years now.

Keegan wrote and published his first novel, titled; How I Make My Bed in Hell.

He wrote his first fictional and nonfictional story amongst many, before his disability occurred, and never had a chance to publish it because of his physical and mental situation. But now, his family and team helped him make this happen.

He is out of work due to his mental and physical disability, and still under treatment.

HI THERE!

How are you managing life this day? I am glad that you finally reach the last part of this book. Thank you for taking time to flip through this topic, and I hope that I did not undermine your moralities, nor your principles.

By the way, did someone tell you that you look glamorous while reading?

I love the way you changed your posture just to get the best possible position that you wanted. Even me, sometimes, I have to move from one place to another while being physically sick just to write for you. I truly adore how you are sitting comfortably on the sofa, with your glasses on. I like the way you stand up from the couch, and lay down on your mattress. Perhaps, you're tired of the location.

I understand that you took your time to rest, or to do something, but in the end, I am grateful that you opened this book again, and continued where you stopped. This time you are sitting in one of your quiet and peaceful places in your home, with a cup of coffee on your hand. Your place could be your veranda facing your beautiful garden that is full of flowers, and the birds are singing as your mind reads every word. The wind is embracing you, and the sun is cheering you up to read.

A wonderful day indeed.

This book is never meant to attack your belief and your culture. It is my perception. I know that you understand that I am only doing this because I want other people to open their eyes about the things on earth. I want them to be knowledgeable when it comes to the darkness of the world.

I hope that I planted useful things in your life, and not confusion. Your opinion matters to me; you are free to give your impression with this creation. I will not let you feel that I am attacking you. I am here to write what is true, and only true.

May this book brings not agony but serenity.

Your partner in seeking truth,
Keegs

www.ingramcontent.com/pod-product-compliance
Ingram Content Group UK Ltd.
Pitfield, Milton Keynes, MK11 3LW, UK
UKHW042003190726
13854UKWH00005B/2142